AF413166

GOD IS BIGGER

GOD IS BIGGER

Than The Mountain You Are Facing

RUSSELL L. ESTES

This book is dedicated to
RACHEL SHANEYFELT
and all those out there
who have been affected by cancer.

www.gibmovement.com

"For with God nothing shall be impossible."
Luke 1:37
KJV

CONTENTS

PREFACE

We all need to know that when life gets big, God is BIGGER.

In 2011, Rachel Shaneyfelt was diagnosed with mesothelioma, a rare asbestos-related cancer, and given only nine months to live. She was in nurse practitioner school when she was given this death sentence but decided to get her degree anyway . . . and that she did.

While working as a nurse practitioner, she was scheduled for a lung biopsy. They wouldn't do the procedure because the size of the lesion had drastically diminished! She later told a doctor, "You're not going to believe this, but my lesion has shrunk 70 percent. Praise God!"

The doctor, who was an atheist, said, "That's great, get yourself a T-shirt."

So, that's what she did. She bought 130 "God Is Bigger" T-shirts and gifted them to nurses and staff. And with that, the God Is Bigger Movement was founded.

To continue spreading the Word, Rachel purchased 1,000 "God Is Bigger" silicone bracelets, designed to draw attention to the solution —*not* the problem.

Rachel challenged her small group to take and give them to total strangers. In one week, the bracelets were gone. Within months, the demand for bracelets went global. By 2014, Rachel could no longer provide bracelets for free, and she started distributing GIB apparel for a donation.

Additionally, the God Is Bigger Movement has an annual fundraiser for the sole purpose of raising money to continue the movement. To date, with the proceeds from GIB merchandise and their annual fundraiser, the God Is Bigger Movement has distributed over 800,000 bracelets worldwide.

Although merchandise is available for donation, the GIB Movement gives a large portion of its inventory to missionaries in and out of the country, charities, flood and fire victims, the homeless, victims of mass shootings, outreach ministries, refuge centers, human trafficking victims, and anyone suffering a loss.

The God Is Bigger Movement provides a banner of hope for those hurting or lost. Wherever we see the need, we go and we give. There are countless stories of how these bracelets have changed lives during times of hardships. Whether that need is for healing; saving a marriage; getting a job; overcoming grief, addiction, or depression, God *will* meet our needs.

On August 26, 2017, Rachel Shaneyfelt went home to be with her Savior. Rachel was a strong, courageous woman and a huge inspiration to so many. She will forever be missed.

It was Rachel's wish that the God Is Bigger Movement carry on. Her family and friends will continue the Movement in her honor to bring glory to God to show that He is and will always be BIGGER.

INTRODUCTION

Before you read this poor excuse for American literature, I need to ask you a question: *"Have you ever cried out to God and asked why He gave you exactly what you asked for?"*

I bet you're scratching your head over that one. You're also probably wondering what my answer is. I could tell you, but we would have to wrap up this book on page one, and that wouldn't make for a good read. My editor would probably turn in her two-week notice right here on word number ninety.

So, let's avoid all that. Let's work together: I'll keep writing, and you keep reading and leaving me awful reviews. Just know that once you go past this point, we're a team until the pages fall out of this book.

Great! Welcome aboard. We're practically cousins now. I apologize.

In my previous books, I touched on the importance of letting God lead us and guide us. Now I want to expand on that.

We know that life can throw curveballs at us out of the blue. Without something or someone to turn to for help in times of turmoil, it would be easy to give up, to throw in the towel, or perhaps even wonder if our lives are worth continuing. Thus, the case with me this past year when the dreadful C-word found its way into my body, catching me off guard.

2 Corinthians 5:7 tells us it can be difficult to trust God during uncertain times but, as believers, we know *His* ways are not *our* ways. Both **Isaiah 55:8-9** and **Romans 8:28** say that ultimately, He will work *all* things for good.

What does that mean for us? Having faith and trusting Him in difficult times allows you to find peace in God's presence.

As we go through our daily lives, each one of us experiences difficult situations. Many times, when we go through pain or suffering, we're surprised these situations have found a way into our lives. We forget God told us we *will* experience hardships, but He's already given us the gift of faith and taught us to use this valuable fruit of the Spirit. However, many of us do not. In difficult or confusing times, we're quick to worry instead of practicing trust and faith.

The grace of God gave us the gift of faith—not because we deserve it but as a result of the everlasting goodness of His works. It's also important to know that this gift we've been given is not in exchange for us accomplishing good works. Appreciation for this gift should fill our hearts with humility, knowing we've been given something we could never achieve on our own.

Looking back at the day I got the news about the trespassing cuss word inside my body, trust was something I didn't find a place for in my vocabulary. I uttered words like *pray, bills, feed my dogs* . . . and *I love you*. I had no idea what to expect, but I felt they weren't good things.

I had tried to be a good servant to my Savior but still found myself hearing one of the most dreadful words ever invented. I thought I was healthy; I was happy and enjoying life. I had no idea something inside me was growing that could either change my life or take it. Needless to say, my emotions were everywhere!

At first, I really wasn't sure which one I should let take the lead. Should I be mad? Should I be scared? Nervous? And my kids . . . Would they understand everything about to be thrown my way? Should I feel sadness for them?

There were so, so many more questions. How would my cancer affect my wife? Would there be surgery? Would I have to take treatments, and would they require a port? Could I still work? How sick would I get? Would I . . . die?

Inside, I was a crumpled heap of nerves and emotions, but I had to give the image that the diagnosis was no big deal, and I had to make sure my attitude remained positive.

Still, I worried over how my kids would respond. It was important that my worry never crack their shells. I knew my wife would be right there in the trenches with me, but my children needed to see me just like they always had: strong, protective, and happy. That meant I needed to trust God and to put faith into action . . . even when I wasn't sure what I needed to trust Him to do.

CHAPTER 1

HAPPY NEW YEAR

Fireworks flash overhead! There are loud pops, explosive bursts of colors, and whistling rockets flying across my patio. The street on which I reside looks like Operation Desert Storm.

Our neighborhood association sent out reminders that fireworks are strictly prohibited. *Strictly* was underlined, but they forgot to capitalize the word *prohibited,* so that didn't make it believable.

Inside, we've almost overdosed our Chihuahua on nervous pills and polished off leftover pulled pork and a fried chicken bucket from the Chevron station. The tradition of consuming end-of-year cholesterol by the shovelful is one we've carried on for almost two decades. I've mastered the art of artery-clogging by midnight just so we can start our diets on January 1.

Our television is set to *Dick Clark's New Year's Rockin' Eve* special from Times Square. It's a celebration we always look forward to.

The show has been around since the pilgrims arrived at Plymouth Rock with harpsichords and dulcimers, ready to proclaim the new land and count down the ball drop with the Native Americans. They sang melodies from *The Ainsworth Psalter,* a book published in Holland and brought across the pond with cast-iron pots and flannel underwear. It hasn't changed much over the years, except now the entertainers on stage wear much more revealing underwear and their instruments are powered by a nuclear plant.

At one time, this night was flooded with college football games. Somewhere along the way, the bigwigs looked at the ratings and saw that nobody was watching the games. Everyone was out partying, buying cheap whiskey, and playing their harpsichords. Away went the games; they were moved to the next night . . . except for a couple of low-key games.

For instance, take the one challenging the rockin' Times Square event—two teams I've never heard of: Upper Grand Canyon Institute for Gooder Learning versus the Fighting Okra from the University of Southwest Lexington in the Campbell's Tomato Soup-Stained Tupperware Bowl. Do you see now why we've chosen Dick Clark's musical over such a sure-to-be slobber-knocker of a game?

On the TV, Ryan Seacrest is reading several well-known celebrities' New Year's resolutions off cue cards. One of Nashville's biggest stars claims, "This year, I want to spend more time with my family. I want to make sure they know they are the most important thing to me."

Before he flips to the next card, Ryan says, "I think that's most of us in this business."

Then he reads from a new card: "I need to do better about eating healthy on the road. Just last night, arriving in New York, I ordered a whole pizza for myself and ate it while I was waiting for our dinner to arrive."

The large video display behind Ryan suddenly lights up, and a young hip-hop artist flashes on the screen. She's live. Ryan addresses her and asks how she is. They small-talk and give plugs for her new album and upcoming tour.

"So, what's your New Year's resolution?" he asks.

"My whah?"

"Your *resolution*," he repeats. "You know. What do you want to do better this year than you did last year? Do you plan on eating better? More time with your fans? How do you plan on spending the next 365 days?"

"Uh . . . I dunno. Nobody has told me yet," she says while twisting her hair.

Ryan tries to prompt her. "When we talked earlier, you mentioned something about helping with the homeless situation in your hometown. Is that something near and dear to you?"

She squeals. "Oh, yeah! I almost forgot they told me to say that." She then reaches into her jacket pocket and produces a folded piece of paper and opens it. "This year, I, like, wanna do, like, more charity work. Like, actually getting out, and like, y'know, working and stuff. But not, like, too much. And not on weekends. And I'll need, like, an assistant to actually do this for me."

Ryan continues. "The homeless situation is growing rapidly across America. Do you have an idea of how we can change that?"

"Yeah. Totally," she tells him.

Silence.

Ryan furrows his brow.

More silence.

"Can you share that?" he asks.

"Like, there's way more homeless people than there, like, used to be. So, like, in order to fix this, we should, like, tell them to, like, buy themselves a house or something."

Ryan tilts his head and stares at her like a confused Labrador. "We will be right back after these messages."

As I dust potato chip crumbs from my shirt, I turn to look at my wife, Kristy. "We should make a resolution."

"Like what?" she asks. "Eating better?"

"Nah. I'm already good at that," I proudly proclaim. "You know, like, maybe start walking daily. Maybe do a date night at least once a month."

"You mean things we will never do." She smirks. "Besides, I thought you hated resolutions."

She's right. I hate them with a passion.

Why would I want to give myself another reason to fail? I already have many opportunities to fail, and they usually find me without me adding any more. But still, here I am, trying to add punishment to my life. Everything seems hunky-dory yet I want to pile on some crazy idea called a resolution to change it all. Why was this crazy thing invented?!

The psychology behind New Year's resolutions is faulty. They're supposed to be something to get excited about. Something that could potentially change our lives. They usually don't. Resolutions can't lead to sustainable behavior change because they aren't constructed in a way that harnesses motivation and turns it into action and change.

Sure, you may have some guy with chiseled abs profess to drink more water this year and actually succeed, but most of us will have brownie crumbs in our beards by midday January 2. We're all bound to fail to lose that weight, get to inbox zero, exercise more, clean out the junk drawer, stop drinking so much, or feel more gratitude. And because resolutions don't work, they are inherently depressing.

By one estimate, 80 percent of resolutions are abandoned by February. Interestingly enough, that's about the time anti-anxiety pills are in such high demand that pharmaceutical companies have to activate their third shifts.

Making New Year's resolutions sets you up to feel like a failure, a loser, a lazy person, or a Cleveland Brown's fan. Paradoxically, *because* you fail so quickly and thoroughly (have you ever resolved to lose weight and then pigged out five hours later at a New Year's Day football-watching party?), you easily give up trying to change.

New Year's resolutions typically involve one of three wishes:

1. To stop avoiding something (like getting rid of all the charging cords that no longer work).
2. To stop doing something that makes you feel unnaturally good (such as overeating or drinking, smoking, or binge-watching reality TV).
3. To start doing something that doesn't come naturally (like journaling, expressing gratitude, exercising, or speaking in a non-redneck tone).

My wife was right. Resolutions make me mad, depressed, and broke.

I can pledge to lose ten pounds by March and spend $2,000 on vitamins and supplements to reach that goal. Just think—that's $200 a pound! I'm top-shelf Wagyu beef!

These days, we just sit at home and watch people in skinny britches and sparkly outfits scream into microphones as we observe our front yard explode with bottle rockets, whistlin' chasers, and roman candles. I'm pretty sure there's been at least one Sherman tank sound off at the end of my driveway. At one time in our life, Kristy and I went out to celebrate the new year. As kids came along, our joints ached, and bedtime came at sundown, we eliminated parties and clubs.

Don't get me wrong, we had some fun times back when we were young and carefree. At a restaurant and bar one New Year's Eve, the lead singer of the band onstage looked at his watch and shouted, "It's time to get ready. We're gonna count this down! At the stroke of midnight, I want every husband to be standing next to the person who made your life worth living."

The bartender was almost crushed to death by people rushing to be by his side as the confetti dropped. I don't need that in my life. It's too dangerous!

I quickly learned I would rather spend the time at home with my family. I want to reach milestones with them. I often feel guilty if I do fun things without all my tax deductions there. If we're together during the big moments in life, such as ringing in the new year, opening Christmas gifts, or shouting Baptist cuss words at Talladega, we will always have a bond that holds us together.

We used to do game nights. Family game night is a time-honored tradition in many households. It's a chance for families to come together and bond over pizza and threats to put up smartphones, *or else!*

Monopoly can change an entire family for life. Spouses are sometimes lost over charging double rent on Boardwalk. But it does one thing that I enjoy: puts everyone within hugging distance.

On this particular night, I'm proud that my wife talked some sense back into me. I knew better than to even think about a resolution. Why would I want to endure such punishment? Instead, I'll do the one thing that's gotten me through all the other stupid moments in my life. I'll pray.

Walking out onto my front lawn, I look up at the gazillion stars and bottle rockets. I'm not sure what I'll be praying for, so I just start talking to God.

I could spend the next three hours simply thanking Him for what He's done for me in just the last few days. I could also ask Him for blessings, or perhaps thank Him for the ones I already have—you know, the *essential* stuff: food, shelter, and fishing tackle. I need to ask favors for some of my friends. Some are hurting. Some are sick. Some aren't Alabama football fans. I could talk to Him about a lot of stuff . . .

But I know there's a line already forming, and I don't want to hold everyone up. Instead, I'll make it short.

"God, I know you've got bigger fish to fry than to listen to me, but just hear me out. I have a long track record of screwing up, so resolutions are probably something I don't need to partake in, but I just think I need a year that will change me.

I'm in a slump. I need something that will open my eyes to the things I've become complacent about. I don't know why I feel like this could be the year, but I believe in big things, and I believe that I'm due one.

Lord, please use this upcoming year to do something big in my life that glorifies YOU.

Amen."

CHAPTER 2

WHAT IN THE WORLD IS THAT?

"Honey, have you seen my belt?"

"I can't believe you're asking me. It's right where it always is," Kristy yells from the kitchen.

"Where?!"

"It's hanging on your belt hanger—on your closet door," comes her response, more agitated for some reason.

"No, the brown one. This is the black one."

"*Behind* the black one."

My wife and I engage in this dance, a common couple's tango, no less than three times per week.

Replace "belt" with any number of other household items and it's the same conversation, sometimes argument, about how I can't find anything—because she moved it!—because I don't look hard enough . . . because she moved it. It's yet another reason why I can't live without her. I don't know where she puts anything.

When I go to look for a stamp, a certain shirt, or that bottle of ketchup that's lived on the second shelf of the fridge door for two years, I don't know where she's moved it to. Of course, if I dare ask, she'll cue the same line that spouses for all of eternity have been spewing to their significant others. I'm sure cave people did the same.

Cave-wives would holler at their cave-husbands and tell them they couldn't find the big rock used for killing their dinner if it were on their head. Cave-husbands would holler back and ask where their cave-wives moved it to.

Cave-wives would then shriek, "It's in the second drawer of the hutch, just like it's been for the last 2,000 years! When are you going to stop asking me?"

Men have a well-known reputation for looking for something for eight-one-hundredths of a second before screaming for their wives to point it out, usually about eye level two feet from them. It comes from years of placing tools right back where we got them from.

Husbands tend to need their wives more than wives need their husbands. It's a fact of life I have known ever since I was a child observing my parents.

Most of the time, it's pretty obvious that men would be useless without their partners. That's usually what motivates them to finally marry in the first place. One day, they give up on trying to find the spare key to the truck; the next minute, someone takes their last name, goes straight into the kitchen, and gets the key out of the junk drawer.

You know the saying: If a man's brain wasn't attached to his head, he wouldn't know where to find it. We have no idea where anything is, even if it's staring us in the face, right behind the black belt. Children tend to have this problem, too. Wives and mommies never do. Watching them do it is amazing.

They can tell you exactly where in the back of the closet you'll find the feather duster you haven't used in four years and five months. They know it's been that long, too. Without them, we wouldn't be able to find our own feet, let alone the car keys or important documents and the like.

It goes beyond scavenger hunts. Sometimes, we have no earthly idea how things get done around the house.

For instance, some of us men—not all—have no idea how the laundry gets done. We throw our dirty clothes on the floor just beside the hamper and miraculously, everything ends up clean, neatly folded, and organized in our drawers and closets. It's like some laundry fairy just *poofs!* it all into existence. Little do most of us know that the saintly creation from one of our ribs is, in fact, the laundry fairy.

Hence, the belt that is avoiding me, the very one Kristy has now come and pointed to while giving me *that* look. And, of course, she gives me the business about "actually looking" before hollering like somebody went and set my britches on fire. She hastily walks back out of our master bathroom and leaves me holding my belt. I don't have time to tell her I can't find my crimson button-up shirt that I reserve for important meetings.

I know I shouldn't rely on clothing for luck, but it's the shirt I wore when Alabama won the conference championship. I had it on when I won the prize basket at the school fair. It was also the shirt I just happened to be wearing the day I walked into the Piggly Wiggly and learned their coolers were out and they had to quickly reduce their meat stock. I got six packs of thick sliced bologna for the price of one *and* a family pack of neck bones for fifty cents a pound. Tell me this shirt ain't lucky and I'll show you a bologna sandwich fit for Dale Earnhardt.

Instead, I'm standing in defeat, still clutching my belt and holding a blue shirt. I've already gone over my options and chose this route as opposed to asking my wife for help again. Men can think and calculate decisions quicker and better than we get credit for. How else could we have lived this long after the invention of power tools?

Men can climb sixty-foot ladders with fifteen different power tools tied to them and not worry about anything because they're wearing safety glasses. Just barely a hundred years ago, men hadn't evolved enough to make such safely oriented decisions. But look at us now! We have enough power tools to build twelve replicas of Noah's ark and still have both eyes. Most of us.

I'm sliding on my Carhartt's and getting ready to conquer the day. Right about the time the waistline of my britches rubs against my upper hip, just about where the scavenger hunt belt will reside, I hit something that causes me to wail like a wounded deerhound. It feels like a hot coal poker has just been introduced to my hindquarters.

So, I do what I'm supposed to do as a member of the male species: I poke the area with my finger, and—

I come unglued again! This hurts worse than the time I got a fishhook stuck in my belly button (another story for another day).

I lower my pants just below the beltline and turn so I can get a better look in the mirror. There's a small spot, maybe the size of a pencil eraser. It's discolored, but it doesn't stand out too bad. It's like a freckle on steroids, raised just a tad from the surrounding tissue. I've never noticed it before.

So . . . I poke it again.

Yep! Still hurts.

Less than a minute into this battle, I've already learned that this thing is painful.

See! I told you we men are smart. Now I know what *not* to do.

I turn a little more and use a small handheld mirror to gain an even better view, and . . . Well, I poke it again. Pain shoots deep inside my hip and lower back. I didn't say our memories were great.

My Carhartt britches are at half-mast now, and my gluteus maximus is facing the mirror. I'm twisted about as much to one side as I can get without requiring an orthopedic visit, trying my best to get a good view of this newly found torture button. I raise onto my tiptoes, risking copays and deductibles, and this is the time my wife decides to come back into the master bath.

Kristy looks at me. I look at her. I smile. She doesn't.

"Proud of that thing, huh?" she asks.

I spin my hindquarters in her direction. "Take a look at this!"

"I've seen it before," she replies. "Nothing to brag about."

"I've got a little knot here. I can't see it well enough to make out anything."

Kristy takes a peek. I point it out. She presses it with her finger. I commence to hollering again.

"I've already done that!" I squeal. "It don't help!"

"I don't know, babe. Maybe you should get that looked at," she responds as she pokes it again.

I yell things a third-generation Baptist should not. I've heard these things come from a Presbyterian on the bottle but never a sober Baptist. I instantly go to the Lord in prayer and ask Him to give me a temporary suspension and not kick me out of the club entirely. I even offer up the money I've been saving for a new Shimano fishing reel as tithes if He'll just act like this never happened.

Here I am, just two weeks into the new year, and I already have a reason to see a doctor . . . and I am *not* good with doctors.

I'd rather Google my symptoms and then turn in my notice to my employer because the world wide web told me I had two and a half hours to live. Like most men, I brush illness off. My preference is to buy eight dollars' worth of over-the-counter medication than spend the ten bucks on my insurance deductible and get a shot.

Doctors just make me nervous. I become faint and nauseous during even very minor medical procedures, such as making an appointment by phone. I guess I'm like most of the guys out there. I also guess this could be a deciding factor on why women live longer than men. I just hate going.

My dad used to say it was a waste of money. "A hospital bed is a parked taxi with the meter running," he'd yell while duct taping a finger back on.

I think it's normal to feel bad every now and again. It's how our immune systems grow and adapt to new things. I get sick a couple times a year, and my wife will holler at me to go get checked out. I stand my ground and just like I tell her, I get better. It may take six weeks, but I'm better.

I think I'm more afraid of what they might find. Will I get a diagnosis that locks me inside for weeks? Will it require surgery? Will they put me to sleep? What if I don't wake up?

General anesthesia is so weird. You go to sleep in one room, then wake up four hours later in a totally different room. Just like in college. But I'm past all that. Why go back?

I WRESTLE with the notion for a few days before making the call. I really don't want to go in and see my regular doctor. I just want someone to look at this bump on my rump. If I see my regular guy, he'll fuss at me about my cholesterol, lack of exercise, and the annual checkup I haven't had in three years. I don't need that kind of negativity in my life. I just want to wear britches again without this knot hurting.

I decide a dermatologist is the best route, so I look one up close by and dial the number. It takes two times. As soon as the receptionist answers the phone the first time, I hang up and hyperventilate. Too nervous to call back, I wait until later in the day. She answers again.

"Hello! It's a beautiful day at Dermatology Associates," she says in the politest voice ever created. "How may I help you?"

Silence. I can't catch my breath. Why is this so difficult? Then I start breathing harder.

"Hello," she repeats. "Hello?"

"Hey . . . Ummm. Hi." I'm a mumbling idiot. *Just tell her why you want to come in.*

"Can I help you?" she asks.

"Yes!" I reply quickly before I change my mind.

Silence.

"Okay. Well, how may I help you?"

I go through the whole spiel. I tell her I need to see a doctor and why. She gives me options for new patients. I pick a date. This is going better than I thought. Then—

"Now, where exactly is this spot that concerns you?"

I've just met this lady! I can't talk about my . . . you know, *that* area! It's not how my momma raised me. Back in the day, I shook my money-maker like I had spare parts without a care who saw. But now, I can't even talk to this lady about "the spot."

"It's just above my knee," I tell her.

"Okay. Left or right side?" she wonders.

"Right."

"Front or back?"

She sure is asking a lot of questions. Can't I just tell all this to the doctor?

"Back," I say.

"Okay, so the back of your right thigh," she replies. "Got it."

Hesitantly I whisper, "Well, not exactly."

"Excuse me? Is that not correct, sir?"

"Well, it's a little higher than the thigh."

"Okay. No problem. Let me change this. Now, where *exactly* is it?"

I give her another hint: "It's a little lower than my mid-back."

She keeps prying. "So, would you say lower back?"

"About where my belt goes. Maybe a little lower."

"So, it's on your butt . . .?"

And there it is. It's out there.

I just met this lady five minutes ago and we're talking about my butt. I'm going straight to Hades or possibly even Chicago. It's a good thing we're connected only by cellular waves because my face is about the shade of Crayola number FC2847: Scarlet Red.

"Umm. Kinda. It's more on my hip," I offer as a condolence. "Maybe upper buttock region. I'm really not sure about the medical terminology for this area. I wouldn't necessarily call it my . . . my butt. Maybe it's like the extended lower hip but on the back side of the hip. I didn't do well in anatomy. It's not that I was stupid or anything. Not all the way. It's just that I didn't think I would need to know this information after tenth grade. I have a friend that passed that class, and he was a goof at algebra, too. And—"

"Sir? Sir!" she interrupts. "It's okay. I have you down, and the doctor will see you next Tuesday."

"Okay! Great. What all should I bring?"

"Just you, your insurance card, and your butt."

CHAPTER 3

NO BIG DEAL

Do you ever have those days that just slowly creep by? That's how most of mine go, but not the days after I make my appointment.

There were only six days that separated that phone call and me from showing my rear end to a stranger, and they have all flown by like a weeklong-free Netflix trial. I want to cancel the appointment, I'm past the twenty-four-hour window needed to avoid a fee before I know it.

If there's anything I dislike more than doctor's appointments, it's wasting money. Those two things have been in a fight all week with each other. Like most things in this world, decisions are made by prayer and bank accounts.

So, on the day of the nervous breakdown, otherwise known as the appointment, I get up and start my day just like any other—with enough coffee to caffeinate an entire carnival crew and reading the Good Book. I take my daily dose of life juice and head outside on my patio to talk to the Creator of the universe while watching my favorite wonder of each day: the sunrise.

The sun pours through the trees lining our property. Another day has dawned, bringing with it new hopes and aspirations. It's not rare that I'm up at this time of the morning. I usually get up in time to wake the birds, make the rooster crow, and scare the raccoons out of our trash. It's a ritual. I have an internal clock that thinks if the sun rises while I'm still in bed, the entire world may just up and explode like an overheated spray paint can.

This particular morning stands out. I don't know why.

Maybe God knows I'm as anxious about this appointment as a cat with a bottle rocket tied to its tail, so He's done me a solid and delivered a beautiful start to the day. The morning air is so fresh, and there's not a sound in the world.

Waking up early gives me a chance to witness one of the true beauties in the world. It all happens before the world wakes, and a sunrise like this one is something everyone should witness in their lives. The way the world stops in that moment gives such peace within me to take on the day. Every sunrise offers a new beginning, a new chance to start over, and a new day we learn to appreciate.

I have always found **Luke 1:78-79 (ESV)** to be one of the most beautiful verses in the Bible:

> *"because of the tender mercy of our God, whereby the sunrise shall visit us from on high to give light to those who sit in darkness and in the shadow of death, to guide our feet into the way of peace."*

Wow! Read that one more time. Do you see it? The very sunrise we see is the promise of God Himself.

The reviving light of the knowledge of the glory of God can only be seen in the face of the Lord Jesus Christ, for He is the Dayspring from on high. He is history's unique Person. He is the Morning Light of God's grace. He is the reviving Light Who alone gives life, hope, peace, and love.

Yes, Jesus Christ is the Morning Star. He is the coming Son in Whom is Light and Life—eternal life, abundant life. His Light and Life continue to be shed abroad through the light of the glorious gospel of saving grace to all who will believe in His name.

Hallelujah . . . Praise Him . . . Glorify Him . . . Whew! I need to sit down for a minute.

On a day like today, when I'm nervous, scared, and about to give up that no-show fee, God reminds me: "Hey, big guy. I am here with you. Don't be afraid. Walk in that office today and show your butt to that man like it ain't no big deal."

Well, maybe those aren't His exact words, but they're what I need to hear.

As the sun continues climbing, I know God has orchestrated all this for me. Sure, the entire hemisphere can see it, but it is *mine,* a masterpiece He's painted for me.

No. It's more than that.

A masterpiece provides a simple but beautiful way for anyone to express their skills. For hundreds of years, masterpieces have been sought after and praised. From the priceless paintings of famous artists like Picasso, Banksy, and Basquiat to the construction paper art hung on refrigerator doors by proud moms and dads, each is beautiful.

But this . . . this is more. It is breathtaking! It's soul renewing!

Every masterpiece from a highfalutin artist is protected by the Securities and Exchange Commission, providing a form of investor protection and transparency even when compared to similar investments in other physical assets like gold. They are stored in a climate-controlled secure facility located somewhere like Delaware, Rome, or the U-Haul storage down the road.

But not the masterpiece I'm seeing.

Though I believe it to be mine, it is on display for everyone. It's free of charge. It carries a unique message for all.

To some, it says, "You made it! You're alive to see this again."

For me, it says, "Man-up and go see the doc."

And that's enough.

A FEW HOURS LATER, I find myself sitting in my truck outside the dermatology clinic. I'm nervous. Again.

God had prepared me just earlier but, like the coffee, all that prepping has worn off, and I am (again) contemplating going back to the office without getting checked out. I sit here and use my smartphone to self-diagnose. It tells me I have everything from an infected hair follicle to a reaction to the poisonous dart frog species from the Amazon basin.

As I ponder the question of whether I should even get checked out, I do what I always do when I feel like this. I talk to God.

I imagine He's sitting with me, riding shotgun in my Chevy pickup. He has on His Alabama baseball cap and his Sea of Galilee flip-flops. We're listening to country music. The good kind. Not this new stuff with all the squealing and hollering about tractors by guys that can't start a lawnmower. I turn down Willie Nelson and look over at Him.

"God? I hope it's okay I call you that. Should I call you Mr. God? Creator? Master? Father? I'm more than happy to address You in any manner You wish. But here's the deal: I don't have a good feeling about this. I don't even want to go in, but I'm going to. I know if I go back home and tell my wife I chickened out, she won't take it too kindly. She'll holler at me in ways You won't approve of. So, if You would, give me peace about this . . . and whatever we find in there today, just walk with me along the journey. I promise to do whatever with it You intend. I appreciate You, God. More than I show."

Then, I turn off Willie, open my truck door, and slowly start toward the clinic. I pause just before entering as if to second guess my choice. Instead, I trust God, and I step inside.

I spend the next twenty minutes filling out forms. They want to know everything about me: family, ancestors, what type of motor oil I use. Everything. Once finished, I load it all into a wheelbarrow and return it to the front desk.

Finally, my name is called. I'm led down a series of hallways with turns and doors. There's no turning back now. I couldn't find my way back out if I tried.

I'm assigned a room and sit in a plastic chair as if waiting for my trial to begin. As the smell of antiseptics and medicine fills my nostrils, I scan my surroundings and see that the room looks strangely green. Posters of skin rashes and oddly shaped freckles hang all around me.

I want to get a quick glance at my spot and start doing my own diagnosis, but I don't have time—there's a knock at the door. It swings open before I can answer. A short lady that looks like she hasn't hit the legal drinking age steps into the room wearing a wide smile. She's holding a piece of blue and white fabric.

"Mr. Estes?"

"That's me."

"The doctor wants you to remove all your clothing and put this on."

She hands me a gown about the size of a washcloth.

"Everything?" I ask.

"Everything," she confirms.

"Even my . . .?"

"Yep, even those."

I strip down to what I would normally wear to take a shower and sit back down on the chair, which now has become the same temperature as Blue Bell Rocky Road. I shift myself, pulling my washcloth under me to keep my taillights from freezing to the chair. And I wait. Some more.

I look around the room again and am surprised to see that it's quite merrily decorated even though I'm trying to ignore the posters promoting the dreaded C-word. I mean, after all, that's *not* what I have. I have a weird freckle that, for some reason, became sore and swollen.

Another knock.

This is it. Game time!

The doctor enters and introduces himself. He makes small talk to calm me. I guess the sweat beading up on my forehead is an indication that I'm wound up tighter than an eight-day clock.

He has the posture of a soldier. Every action he takes is precise and purposeful. He smiles in the cold and distant way professionals do. It says, "I care about you, but I'd rather be golfing."

I can never relax around such expressions. I need a genuine face, preferably a smile but if not, I'd really rather a person not fake it. I feel like this guy wears a fake smile. Maybe it isn't. Maybe he just knows he's about to have to look at the open portion of my gown and he's as excited about it as I am.

"So. You have a spot on your rump that you're worried about, huh?" he asks.

"Well, more like my hip," I reply.

"My papers say right buttock."

"It's a little higher. About the beltline area."

Here we go again. Why is it so hard for a man to call out his own butt?

We go through a series of questions and statements. He uses words I'm not prepared for. Then, things start to get real!

He slips on latex exam gloves and instructs me to stand and lean slightly forward, resting my elbows on the exam table. His assistant hovers behind him like an umpire at a little league game. Guess she's positioned herself for the best view of the show.

"Ah, yeah," the doc says. "There it is."

This worries me. He found it quickly without me pointing it out. It's not like it's the only freckle living in that particular neighborhood. There are quite a few. It's like a star map back there. A whole constellation even. Maybe a galaxy! He's making me nervous.

Say something else, Doc, I think to myself. *What do you think?*

Throughout the examination, he gives commands rather than requests. The assistant lingers two feet behind, her earlier relaxed expression replaced with knitted brows and a grim slash for a mouth. He tenderly touches the mole he spotted as the likely suspect and comments, "I don't think this is malignant, but you need to have it removed immediately."

Immediately? This doesn't sound good at all. "Immediately" is for things like toothaches, flat tires, and allergy medication in the spring.

He pauses before adding in a hushed voice, "Not that I want to worry you."

When someone says those words, the next words do, in fact, worry you. I brace myself for what might come next.

When the prodding is over, the doctor stands back and tells me to have a seat. It *must* be bad. No one ever tells you to sit for good news.

Sitting is for bad news. Sitting is for when you've failed a grade, lost a job, or your transmission has to be put down.

"What is it, Doc?" I ask.

"Well, I'm not sure. We need to cut that off and biopsy it," he says matter-of-factly.

"Biopsy? You think it's cancer?"

"I don't think so," he says, easing my nerves. Some. "But we need to make sure. It is kind of abnormal and appears to be more under the skin than on it."

"But it could be," I ask again.

"Yeah, I suppose it could be a melanoma," he continues, "but even if it is, we can get that out rather simply, and you can go on about your life."

At this moment, I don't know precisely what melanoma is, but I do know the word to which it is most associated: cancer. That alone scares the bejeebers out of me.

I know cancer kills people. I've read stories about how it devastated families, bank accounts, and fishing trips. I've seen cancer patients. They looked miserable, like they were fighting for their lives and barely winning. Which, I guess, they were. Cancer is a battle. No, a war!

The "war on cancer" has been a dominant theme since the early 1970s when President Nixon announced a national commitment to vanquish cancer at the same time the Vietnam War was being fought. With the stroke of a pen, he created funding to help conquer this evil thing.

They thought that should do it. No more cancer, right?

Wrong!

Cancer-battle imagery was so pervasive that in 1978, Susan Sontag wrote the book *Illness as a Metaphor,* which described cancer as an "evil, invincible predator" with "cells that invade the body," patients who are "bombarded" with radiation, and chemotherapy that is "chemical warfare that destroys to save."

Destroys to save . . . almost an oxymoron within itself. It's enough to tell me that I never want to go through something like that.

Although times have changed dramatically since Sontag's book was written, with an increased commitment to patient autonomy and engagement, the language surrounding cancer has not changed. Cancer continues to be the enemy. It continues to pulverize anything in its path. Cancer is a cuss word! It's a good thing I won't be dealing with the cuss word.

"Okay. Let me grab a couple of things, and we will get this procedure underway," the doctor says.

"We're doing this now?!" I holler. "I figured we would discuss it. Talk it over. Check my insurance. I'm here on my lunch break. I've got work to do after a while. People to see. Jokes to tell."

I had come here thinking we would look this freckle over and maybe do a follow-up every six weeks or so. I thought I would go home with pamphlets on sun exposure. Maybe even get some free samples of sunscreen. Now, I'm standing here bare-bottomed while Edward Scissorhands sharpens his pocketknife.

"Well, I need to cut some off to see what it is," he explains. "That's how we biopsy it."

"But today? Like, right now?"

He nods. "Yep. Keep your drawers off."

The doc and his assistant leave the room. I'm still wondering why we're in such a rush. He said he didn't think it was anything to worry about. Is he not telling me everything? Did he see something that concerns him but he's withholding evidence?

I start thinking about all the "what ifs."

What if it *is* cancer? What are the next steps? Are there treatments for melanoma? Will I lose my hair? Can I still eat an unlimited supply of Reese's Cups? They say cancer is fueled by sugars . . . Oh, my gosh! Banana pudding! Will I have to give up banana pudding?

The longer I stay, the worse this gets!

The door swings open again, and the doctor comes back in. His assistant follows, rolling a surgical steel tray lined with enough utensils to confuse a five-star waitress.

"All right," he says. "Ready to get this party started?"

It's hardly a party; more like a torture camp I have to pay to attend. It's worse than being force fed meat-free organic burgers.

"This may sting a little," he tells me, "but it will numb the area so we can cut out what's needed for the biopsy."

We? How big is that knife? Why does it require more than one person to hold this utensil?

"Here goes," he says.

Oh, he lied! It doesn't sting a little. It stings *a lot!*

It feels like I just sat on a nest of ticked-off yellowjackets, and they've attached themselves to my unseen parts. I jump and almost bite clean through my lip.

He goes in again, this time in another spot. Then again. A total of four shots around the spot in question. Then, the numbing medicine starts working. It no longer feels like an insect attack. It's tingling, becoming numb, and the sensation is spreading.

Now I'm standing here with a bleeding lip and it feels like I no longer have a right buttock. You could throw a yard dart at it, and I wouldn't know. Until—

"Okay, here we go," Doc says. He makes a few pokes with the needle again. "You feel that?"

"Nope."

He goes in with the filet knife next.

"Hmm," he says to himself.

What does "hmm" mean? What's happening back there with my unmentionables?

"Everything good, Doc?"

"Yeah. Just a little deeper than I thought."

Now he's digging for tenderloins like he's butchering the first deer of the season. I think there're power tools involved at this point. His assistant wipes sweat from his forehead while I squirm like a mouse with its tail caught in a trap.

"All right! Got all I can get," he says. "It is much deeper than I thought, but I got enough to biopsy."

"What does that mean, Doc? Is that bad?" I ask.

"I still think it's malignant," he offers, "but we will know for sure in a few days."

"Should I be worried?"

"Nah. I don't think it's no big deal."

CHAPTER 4

HAPPY BIRTHDAY

Fifty years! How did I get here so quickly? What happened? Why do all these places on me hurt? How did the people I grew up with get so old? Am I really planning on celebrating year number *fifty*?

In the months leading up to my fiftieth birthday, I fantasized about how I might celebrate. There were days I allowed my daydreams to go rogue, admittedly fueled by a little back road memory and the blasting soundtrack of my 1980s adolescence.

I envisioned a tour across the south where I'd visit everyone from my youth: teachers, friends, neighbors, coaches, and yard sale entrepreneurs. A box of cassette tapes would ride shotgun while the sounds of Lynyrd Skynyrd, The Eagles, and Aerosmith serenaded me across every mile. At each stop, a choreographed flash mob would encircle me, in which I danced with everyone I'd ever known in chronological order.

I also thought about renting out a huge venue. Maybe have some of my friends who are musicians come and play a tune or two. We'd eat enough barbecue to cause a pork shortage in the southeast. There would be lemonade. Sweet tea. And for the Baptists, we'd have Pabst Blue

Ribbon and Bud Light longnecks. I'd even invite millennials and whip up kale salads and White Claw seltzers.

As the big day approached, I realized I didn't want any of that. To be honest, I've spent the past few years navigating the challenges of raising kids in a turbulent world.

I had just got my son through college, and he was embarking on real life in a world stacked up against him on all sides. My daughter was caught in the high school trap that can make or break a kid, so we started homeschooling her to provide better opportunities. We were living on a landmine of uncertainty, where the brutal days outnumbered the peaceful ones, and it often seemed as if we were a family in crisis.

Crisis has a funny way of pulling at the loose threads in your life. People tend to either take a few steps closer or a couple steps back, while others—some of whom you'd least expect—run for the hills. Frankly, I can't say I blame them, but it can be terrifically lonely as you run from everything you're afraid of.

As my birthday approached, I mostly wanted to hibernate. I sometimes fantasized about running away to my southern back road tour with my cassette tapes, but that wasn't really in the cards.

My wife kept asking how I wanted to celebrate, and I kept putting her off. I wanted to stay forty-nine for at least a few more years. Fifty just seemed to be the dividing line between where I was and "old people."

To think, in just a week, I would wake up, turn in my "hopes and dreams" card, and realize none of them would ever happen because . . . Well, I'd be fifty, and fifty is too old for dreams to come true.

Let me back up a moment to say that fifty is a gasp-inducing *Twilight Zone* age. Weren't my former teachers that age? I had no problem with my friends turning fifty, but how was it happening to me?

If you know me, you know that I'm a very childlike person. My personal style is *Toddler Who Dresses Himself*. I have intentional bed head. I am full of adventure. I still live with wild abandonment, but I'll stop in the middle of two-lane roads to move a tortoise out of harm's way. If Indiana Jones and Mr. Rogers had a child, it might as well be me.

As ambivalent as I felt about my fiftieth birthday, however, I knew I wanted to mark it in some meaningful way. What did I want for my birthday? What did I need? In digging in as deeply and authentically as I could, I woke up one morning and typed the words I wanted to send to a select group of folks:

I am turning fifty on February 8.

I am twelve on the inside, so I'm not even sure how this is possible. I've given a lot of thought as to how I want to spend the day. I've decided I'm not in the mood for a party. And there is nothing material I need.

What I could use right now is a little booster of love. So, that is why I'm writing to you today.

I'm not sending this to everyone I know. In fact, I'm sending it to just a handful of you. If you are getting this, it means you make my heart beat with fondness and joy. Some of you I know better than others, and some of you maybe I've lost a little touch with, but I am grateful for all of you.

What I'm asking for is a little written something—email me, text me, post on my social media, whatever way you choose—like a story, a memory, how we met, or maybe something you want me to know. A photo even. I don't want this to feel like work. It doesn't have to be long or literary. You don't even have to do it! You will be just as important to me if you act like you never got this.

I'm going to print these, put them in a box, and read them on my birthday and maybe reread them on days I need them. And I'm going to write back with my own letter to you.

OK, that's it. Thank you in advance.

x Russell

I read it and immediately deleted it, snapping my computer shut.

My inner critic hissed, "How narcissistic of you! Why would anyone want homework just because it's your birthday? Everyone is so busy and overbooked as it is! Who do you think you are exactly?"

If there's one thing I learned before fifty, it's to give this mean voice a juicy middle finger, or, at least, stick my tongue out at it. So, I rewrote my letter. I shortened it to basically saying, "Hey, what's our story? How'd we meet?"

I started adding names to my "send" list. I was thinking maybe ten, possibly twelve folks that I could count on to give me something back. I added forty-seven names. Again . . . **DELETE.**

Instead, I started thinking about those forty-seven people. Why did I choose them over the other eight million folks I know? Were they *my crew*? Were those *my people*? Did I just impulsively, instinctively, mechanically, and spontaneously pick my favorites? If so, why them?

If I'd had a party, the list would have looked very different. A party means people in your current city, demographic, and social orbit. My birthday party guests would range in ages from eight to eighty and span the globe from Alabama to Germany. Every chapter of my life would be represented. There would be scholars eating banana pudding with folks who thought the War of 1812 was fought in the 1990s by people in Mississippi on the History Channel. To me, both types of people would be my favorite because *they are my people.*

Over the past fifty years, I've done some weird crap, cool crap, bad crap—pretty much all the craps you can think of. It's kind of fitting that my life can almost be packaged neatly into decades because I like to make square things fit into round boxes. By doing so, I've fit myself into several different groups of people.

I don't think I was ever your average kid. I was never standout smart, standout pretty, standout funny, or standout talented. But I enjoyed people, and I enjoyed seeing people happy. As I got older, I didn't care if their happiness came at my expense. My entire purpose for existence was to make others happy.

So, there I was. It was the week of the big day, and here's what I was thinking:

Let's not make a big deal out of this. Let's not plan a party, a dinner, or anything that will make someone change their plans for me. Let's just cruise right on by this day like it's President's Day or something.

With that thought, the Lord must have been listening. He helped me with that one. My wife Kristy and my mother-in-law—who lives with us—came down with the dreaded COVID-19 virus.

It was a scary situation. You still couldn't buy bacon at the Piggly Wiggly without masking up and getting counted as you walked in. So, by being exposed to them, I too was quarantined.

All plans were off before they were officially made. I wasn't even mad! Number 5-0 was going to breeze right on by without stirring up dust. I'd get to spend it with my family. We'd be together without a schedule to keep up with, which sounded pretty good to me as long as my family members got to feeling better.

Over the next few days, we used our entire month's worth of Netflix subscription plan. We watched old movies, scary movies, and old movies that were scary. We took walks outside. I met new neighbors that have lived close by for ten years. It was great!

We'd adapted to the new way of life due to the pandemic, and had done so over the last year, but something about those days in quarantine just felt different. Being stuck in our house together at the same time my huge milestone week was occurring made me realize that I'd spent years rushing through life, pressuring myself to get the "right" jobs and attend the "right" events, even if all that status-chasing was making me miserable.

Quarantine forced me to slow down in ways I hadn't since I was a kid. From high school through my twenties, thirties, and even forties, I was constantly on the go; that's most of my life. I always said I was one who liked to be busy, but the last few months of pandemic forced slowdown really called on me to think about what I wanted my life to look like moving forward. I thought for sure that I would be a professional basketball player, astronaut, time traveler, or at least a middle school coach. But those goals seemed far-fetched. Especially coaching.

The time spent with my family during the days leading up to my birthday made me stop and think about things. I was trying to figure out what it would look like to intentionally build space in my life to breathe, reflect, and focus on the most important aspects of life—the people around you who make it all worth it.

Who knows . . . maybe it would take God Himself to force me to slow down.

THE MORNING of my birthday starts out about as routine as it can get. I rise before the sun and start the coffeepot. I like my coffee so strong that it could raise Abraham Lincoln from his grave, and this morning, I've added an extra scoop of dark roast just in case Honest Abe stayed out too late.

As my miracle brew starts spreading its aroma through the house, I walk out back and look for the sun to show itself. Sure enough, there it is: God's promise. A new day and new opportunities.

I walk back in and grab my Bible, pour a cup of high-octane go-juice, and retreat outside to spend a few minutes in His Word before the family wakes up. I have an app on my phone that leads me through devotions that cover a wide range of topics.

This one happens to be on **Proverbs 3:5 (NIV)**:

**"Trust in the LORD with all your heart and lean
not on your own understanding."**

At this time of the morning, I don't yet know the impact this verse is going to make, but it's coming.

Understanding has always been a troubled area for me. Many times in my life I've been asked, "You do understand, right?"

Of course, my answer was always, "Absolutely!"

The only issue was I used the southern spelling, where the *"not"* at the end is silent. I still do.

But this passage from Proverbs . . . Well, I really need it to stick. I have no idea what God is showing me, but I know it's just screaming for me to pay attention.

Here, the term "understanding" is so important that in the Hebrew text, it appears first in the sentence: *"Your understanding, do not lean upon."* This word refers to our ability to observe something, gain insight, and discern as a means of formulating a decision.

Due diligence is, of course, our responsibility. Investigate, seek perspectives, apply logic, and formulate ideas. None of which are my strong suits. I tend to get as confused as a squirrel that fell into a moonshine still. Thank God He knows me and can help me through my spiritual hangovers.

God doesn't ask us to forego planning or to throw ourselves blindly into decisions. He calls us to give greater priority to trusting Him. Let confidence in God's character, power, plans, and past faithfulness be the foundation of all your decision-making as you exercise sound judgment.

To *"lean not on your own understanding"* means that you won't give first priority to your limited perspective. "Lean" is, of course, figurative; meaning to depend upon something. One might lean upon a cane, a wall, or another person in order to remain standing.

The message from Proverbs is: *"Feel completely confident in God, and do not depend upon your own intelligence, insight, or skill to keep you from falling."*

I know a gentleman who suffered a terrible injury from an auto accident, and he was confined to crutches for many long weeks. Several times I found him panting like a dog chasing a whitetail deer. His hands became red and sore from the constant use of his crutches. He discovered that leaning on crutches was exhausting. So is leaning on our own understanding!

If you want to spend an exhausting day, try to work out your problems using only your limited viewpoint. Chase down all the possibilities you can think of. When you inevitably hit a dead end, back up and try a new man-made direction. Eventually, you will run out of ideas as well as energy. Then, if you don't trust in God, you'll have only one option left: worry.

Little do I know that on the morning of my big day, worry will slam me like a professional linebacker. As I finish up my Proverbs devotional, I subconsciously store a little message inside my thick noggin. It's a simple message, one I already know but I'll soon need.

"I am here with you" is the message, and I know that He is.

I WANT to get this day started, but my crew is still snoozing like frat boys on Sunday morning. After another hour, I decide to do the one thing that will break their slumber. I cook bacon.

Hallway doors slowly begin opening. One by one, my family comes to life and greets me with, "Happy birthday!" Before long, everyone is up, bellies are full, and I'm smiling like a possum in a restaurant trash dumpster.

Even though I've stated many times that I do not want any presents, I know they each will have something for me to make the day fun. Just as I suspect, Kristy hands me a huge bag of candy, snacks, and gifts. My pleas for "no gifts" obviously fell on deaf ears. She has a giving heart that can't be held by verbal chains. She gives when she wants to give, which I knew before even asking.

I receive a wonderful drawing from my son—a sketch of one of my favorite photos of us at the beach. I'll later have it framed. My daughter gives me the sweetest card and handwritten note, along with a nice shirt she picked out for me at the mall.

Things are fantastic this morning! *This!* This is just how I want my fiftieth birthday to go!

Lunchtime finds us breaking out something that had to be sent straight from the ovens of Heaven. My two favorite things to snack on in the whole world are brownies and banana pudding, which, if done correctly, is spelled *nanner puddin'*. Kristy contacted a local bakery in town to whip up a creation called banana pudding brownies. Let's just say that I've made a complete fool of myself eating these culinary masterpieces.

I settle into my recliner because there's no way I can continue functioning upright after devouring my birthday treat. I flip on the television and scroll through the programming guide. God must really be getting in on the birthday gift-giving because the first thing I see in the channel lineup is an *Andy Griffith Show* marathon. Six hours of Mayberry!

It's possible I've seen every episode of *The Andy Griffith Show* a dozen times. This show has been known to cure illnesses, depression, and hangovers. There's something about Sheriff Andy Taylor and his trusty sidekick, Barney, that can make you smile just as big as Andy does each time everyone else gets worked up. If the whole town were to catch fire, Andy could walk out into the street, smile, and say, "Now this right 'chere ain't as bad as it looks," and everyone would just go back inside like nothing happened.

The day couldn't be going any better. Gifts, snacks, Andy, and my family. Now we're talking about dinner plans for the evening. I'm thinking of hot wings from my favorite wing joint. Kristy and I are discussing flavor options and antacid medication, then . . . the phone call that will change my world comes.

As I talk to the person on the other end, I realize they're saying something I may need to pay close attention to. I leave the room so Andy doesn't distract me. My face must have told Kristy that something is wrong because she follows.

I stand in our dining room, listening. When the call ends, I take a seat at the table. Horrified at the news, I set the phone down and gaze up at Kristy.

"What is it?" she asks.

"My results came back."

"And?" she says, moving closer.

Her eyes show anticipation. My eyes tell her before my voice does.

"It's cancer."

"Oh, babe . . ."

"They think it's already spread to my lymph nodes," I say, still trying to comprehend everything I've just been told.

"What does this mean?"

"I . . . I don't know," is all I can get out.

What a birthday present.

THE CALL HAS COME on my big day. It's changed everything about it, could possibly change everything about my life, and perhaps even take it. My mind reels.

The doctor also informed me that surgery is needed. "It appears it may have already spread, but we need to confirm. We can start treatments after surgery and see what happens."

See what happens . . . The lump in my throat grows as I think about that statement.

"Why?" Kristy asks. I can see tears developing in her eyes as she looks at me. "You've done nothing but be obedient."

I have no answer other than "I don't know" but I cling to the factual knowledge that God is good regardless.

Tragedies in this life are beyond our understanding of this side of Heaven. I believe Christ is good, and that knowledge sings from the depths of my soul. This nugget of truth is more precious to me than life itself.

I've been taught and recognize that faith is not something we can necessarily see, hear, feel, taste, or touch. It is stepping out of our comfort zones and trusting God—regardless of how we feel emotionally. In times like I'm experiencing now, my faith is what I lean on.

The Bible explains:

"Now faith is confidence in what we hope for and assurance of what we do not see." (Hebrews 11:1 NIV)

Believing!

Do I believe that God will heal me? Yes!

Will it be an earthly healing or one that gives me eternal healing? That's His call, but healing *is* coming!

Whatever the outcome, I have peace with it. I believe God will use this for His glory and He will use me to do His work through it.

I have no clue why He chose me to carry this burden. I've done everything I should. I feel closer to Him than I ever have before. But still . . .

God, I can't figure out what You're doing!

That's my immediate thought after receiving such a discouraging phone call on my fiftieth birthday, a day that should be filled with cake, laughter, and good times. Instead, the doctor on the other end of the call told me something that's made my heart skip.

Years before, God invited me to trade my plans for His. He

whispered a promise to my heart and confirmed it through His Word, wise counsel, and prayer. Believing His promise demanded faith. I said "yes" and followed in obedience.

At first, following God's plan felt exhilarating. My prayer journal read like Mark Twain's grand tale of God's greatness. It was filled with adventure, new things, and blessings I never thought I'd see. Then, the journey began to look different than I'd imagined. The road was filled with more potholes than I'd anticipated, and as I let God direct my steps, it seemed He was leading me to the middle of nowhere rather than in the direction of a promise fulfilled.

I didn't doubt God's presence, but I questioned His plans. My enthusiasm waned. My confidence trembled. On my good days, I felt optimistic and persistent. On my bad days, I felt angry and confused.

And on this evening when a phone call has sunk my hope, I feel helpless and stuck. I wonder why. Somewhere, deep inside, I know that God will use this to not only allow me to grow even closer to Him but to also minister to others who are struggling.

Still . . .

"Could You just show me what You're doing, Lord?" I beg.

I don't know how long I've sat here and waited for the Lord's reply, but I do know there's no flash of lightning illuminating God's brilliant plan. No thundering voice explaining His mystifying methods. Just a quiet thought impressed upon my haggard heart:

Do you want a God you can explain or a God you can extol?

Suddenly, through my haze of fear, I recognize an uncomfortable truth:

A God of infinite majesty can't be measured. A God who unleashes miracles can't be contained. A God whose love is eternal can't be explained.

Perhaps that's why **Ecclesiastes 11:5 (ESV)** reminds us:

> ***"As you do not know the way the spirit comes to the bones in the womb of a woman with child, so you do not know the work of God who makes everything."***

God sees more than we can see. He knows more than we know. He works in ways beyond our comprehension. If we agree to follow Him only when we understand what He's doing, we'll always stop short of experiencing His inexplicable wonders.

So, as I sit here in my dining room, on my birthday, with a head full of questions and a heart frayed with disappointment, I realize we have a choice. We can let the mystery of God bolster our doubt or buoy our wonder. We can drown in self-pity or stand firm and use an adverse situation to scream how wonderful God is. We can get mad at God or praise Him for what He's doing.

Abraham praised God beneath the stars—even though he didn't understand how he'd ever become the father of nations.

David praised God in the wilderness—even though he didn't understand why he was running for his life instead of sitting on the throne.

The Israelites praised God with a mighty shout—even though they didn't understand Jericho's wall would fall without a fight.

And right here, on Day One of this battle, I begin praising God for the cancer because what I do know about Him is far more important than what I don't:

- I know God loves me, and He will never leave me. **(John 3:16; Hebrews 13:5)**
- I know He is for me and not against me. **(Romans 8:31)**
- I know God's Word is true, and His heart is kind. **(Psalm 33:4; Acts 14:17)**

As I lift my head from the table, I lift my praises to Heaven. Gradually, my disappointments shrivel in the shadow of my swelling hope. My tears dry, and I go outside. I walk to the far edge of our backyard and gaze back toward our home. The world before me looks bright with an ethereal glow. Above me, the sky melts into a stunning promise of hope.

I don't understand how He does it, scattering breathless beauty across the horizon every day, but I know this: It is wondrous. Just like

He is. And I trust Him. He will use this unwanted birthday present for something so grand that I won't even know what's happening.

I begin wondering what this all might turn into. That prayer on New Year's Eve comes rushing back to me: "Lord, do something big in my life this year that glorifies You."

That was only a month ago. It was just two weeks after that prayer that the spot was found. Is my upcoming battle the big thing? If so, how can it be used to glorify God?

I know I don't have to understand it. I remember the lesson from my devotion this very morning. All I have to do is trust Him.

That's when I give it—the cancer—to Him.

"Lord, if this is the big thing, if this is what I prayed for, I'm going to need Your help. I don't know what to do with it. I have no clue how to use this to glorify You. But I trust You."

CHAPTER 5

GOD IS BIGGER

I haven't met my oncologist or surgeon yet. The appointment is still days away, but I've already started wondering about everything I'll soon face. I'm as scared as a thirteen-year-old boy at a homecoming dance.

I can't get my mind off the cancer. I can't eat. I can't sleep. It's consumed me!

But . . .

Why is it still controlling me?

I gave it to God. I even felt peace about it before Day One ended. I'm also anxious to know how I'm supposed to use this ordeal to glorify Someone with the ability to snap His fingers and make it go away.

I'm praying so often I've had to up my coverage plan. I feel like I talk to God so much others can't get in. The wait line is growing. I just know that before long, management will shut me down. I see it happening: The Apostle Paul, John the Baptist, and Dale Earnhardt are going to show up at my house and limit my time.

So, I do what eases my heart and mind. I start writing.

It's a coping mechanism I've often used. I wrote some of my best pieces as dementia claimed my mom and she began declining. When my son had major surgery, my writings flowed like the Mighty Mississippi. Writing is my getaway.

Roman Catholics cope by attending Mass for several hours and praying nonstop for days. The Jewish faithful endure by eating record-breaking amounts of food and drinking wine by the barrel. Baptists get back to life by consuming grain, hops, yeast, and water while the great deacon Jack Daniels joins them for a cookout. Everyone has their own way. I write.

Maybe *this* is my thing. Perhaps *this* is how I can glorify God. I still have questions of doubt, and the two biggest ones are: "Why?" and "What if?"

By sharing my journey, others might hear how I'm leaning on God. Maybe if I document the entire battle, someone else will gain hope, faith, and courage. Perhaps they have their own "cancer" they need help with and maybe, just maybe, my battle and story will lead them to Him.

I hope what I write helps someone else, especially other parents. So many people depend on all the parents out there, and it can feel overwhelming. You're tired and emotional, but you have to be strong in front of your kids. You don't want them to worry, and that alone makes it doubly exhausting.

Still, the idea of even having cancer is new to me. I'm an infant in this journey. We're really just days into it. I know I want to write a powerful devotional for others, but I'm losing focus on how to explain things.

As I stare at my screen, the Holy Spirit whispers these words of truth: *"God is bigger."*

That's it! Nothing else. And I have no clue what He's trying to tell me. I have a long history of not having a clue. Just ask my wife, former teachers, or anyone at the hardware store. All I can do is sit with a blank look on my face and wonder, *What comes next?*

It's early morning when I try to attach those words to my story. I'm on my back patio, struggling to comprehend the news broken to us the previous day. My best is given to focusing on my morning devotion, but the doctor's voice clouds my mind—"The biopsy results came back, and it's cancer."

I reach for my phone to look up more on advanced melanoma. This is new to me, and I have no idea about what comes next. Suddenly, something comes over me. I tuck my phone back into my pocket, bow my head, and pray.

Emotions hit me that are uncontrollable! And then, something amazing happens. A peace washes over me, a peace that tells me I don't need to understand any of it. God is bigger than cancer or any other thing I will face. Surgeries, treatments, the financial aspects of this monstrous mountain: God is bigger than it *all*.

This seemingly simple yet profoundly powerful truth hits my heart, and my fear subsides.

God is bigger than anything you will face.

The words echo in my spirit as I feel the weight of fear begin to lift, and the warm presence of my Abba Father surrounds me with His love. It's so simple yet so remarkably powerful!

The enemy would like us to believe that our fear is bigger than our God, but the truth of the matter is that it isn't. In fact, nothing is bigger than our God. Not depression, not failed relationships, not Bigfoot . . . and definitely not cancer.

As **Psalm 147:5 (ESV)** boldly declares:

> ***"Great is our Lord, and abundant in power; his understanding is beyond measure."***

Our God *cannot* be measured. He is great, and greatly to be praised. Fear can be quantified to that of our current circumstance, but God is eternal and triumphs over anything the devil will forge against us.

Because God knows all things perfectly, He knows no thing better than any other thing but all things equally well. He never discovers anything; He is never surprised, never amazed.

It may be one of the simplest ideas I've ever written, but I believe that's the whole point. Fear tries to complicate things. It rears its ugly head to intimidate the children of God into believing it has ground to stand upon, but it doesn't.

The truth is: God is bigger than your fear, your addiction, your finances, or your relationships. He is bigger than any of the mountains you climb. Yes, even cancer!

Now, it's up to me to figure out how to use it. But how?

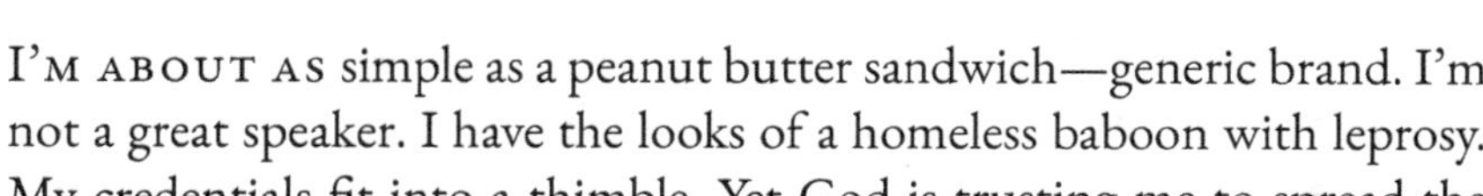

I'M ABOUT AS simple as a peanut butter sandwich—generic brand. I'm not a great speaker. I have the looks of a homeless baboon with leprosy. My credentials fit into a thimble. Yet God is trusting me to spread the gospel through my story.

See, God and I, we made a deal: You walk with me, and I'll go where You lead. So, I write my story.

I write about receiving bad news on my birthday, of the cuss word doctors have thrown at me. I talk about my New Year's Eve prayer, about Scripture, and how faith can get us through anything. I mention bravery, courage, and resiliency, and I post it on social media.

Then I go to bed.

I AWAKE to hundreds of messages the next morning. The post has grown into a storm overnight! I'm bombarded with stories from others dealing with their own mountainous "cancers." Anything from lost jobs to busted radiators.

Throughout the day, my story continues to grow. It continues to be shared. I even receive a message from someone in England who says my message helped them realize they're not alone in their battle. This is just the beginning.

Since I first asked, "Who, me?" God has used this ordinary, backwoods, dirt road, country boy—a simple Christian with nary a credential to his name, a guy with shame in his past and sin in his present—to help others come to Christ. Not only that, but He's also used me to help folks all over the world learn how to have a relationship with Jesus and make Him known to those around them in their everyday lives, their families, workplaces, classes, labs, fantasy football groups, at cookouts, the bar, prisons, their friendships, gaming communities . . . next door to *everywhere.*

And guess what I've learned? Maybe God is using this situation not just to lead others to Him, but perhaps I'm growing closer to Him while doing it.

Even when I thought I was too broken, too simple, and too ashamed, I learned that God can use me, *and you,* to advance His Kingdom to the ends of the Earth. Once we give Him our all, the boundaries are lifted. Our chains are broken.

You may be asking, "Who, me? I didn't grow up in the church."

"Who, me? I haven't been a Christian for that long."

"Who, me? God could never use someone with my past."

"Who, me? I haven't been to Bible college, and I have no formal ministry training or experience."

"Who, me? I'm just a dad, wife, mother, daughter, sister, kid, grandmother, new Christian, barista, corporate executive, artist, student!" . . . the list goes on and on.

You may simply ask, "What can I do?"

Here's the secret: It's not what you can do but what God can do *through* you.

THE DAY of my first appointment to see my oncologist finally rolls around.

To my knowledge, I'm just meeting the team assigned to me. We'll be discussing upcoming appointments, what my insurance covers, treatment facilities, and which one I prefer using. That's how I see things going, so I tell Kristy there's no need for her to join me. It'll only be a long day of talking and setting up the "real appointments." After all, she's already missed a lot of time in the salon with her clients while off with COVID-19, so she's as busy as a dentist in a chocolate factory.

"Just stay here. Take care of your clients," I tell her. "I'm sure you'll be going with me a whole lot, so it's not like you'll miss anything on this one trip."

Gosh, am I wrong! Little do I know this will be the day I'm told how serious things are.

I arrive early at the Kirklin Clinic at UAB Hospital in Birmingham, Alabama. My appointment time is still an hour away, but I have a habitual habit of being early. I sit in a waiting room full of people of all ages. Some have more wrinkles than my Sunday church britches while others are babies. We're all here to see doctors about some form of cancer. A few have that "cancer look" of smooth scalps and fragile bodies, but even more look just like me—a headful of out-of-control locks and a tad overweight.

But . . .

What does cancer really look like?

Cancer doesn't always stand out like the television shows tell us. It's not all bald heads and lost weight. Sometimes, cancer is tired eyes, depressed thoughts, and smiling through the pain. There are also plenty of times you'd never know a person has cancer. I have no idea what my future has in store for me at this point, but I know I'm going to hold on to my smile for as long as I can.

It's finally my turn. My name is called, and I run up front like I've just been called on the *Price Is Right*. After a brief discussion of how today's event will go, I'm rushed off to the first of many scans and needle pokes of the day. My insurance card is smoking by lunchtime.

After seven hours of experiments that resemble late night TV alien abductions, I'm led to a small waiting room with other people. This is the area where I'll be given my results. I had no idea I'd be getting this information today, so I'm nervous.

I wish Kristy were with me. Had I known, she would have been. Everyone else in the room is clumped together in groups of families and friends. They have support people with them. I sit alone.

It's my turn (again). The doctor asks if I want to grab my family before we begin our discussion. That's the first sign that things are not going in the direction I want them to. I walk into another room and sit across from three people: a surgeon, an oncologist, and a chaplain. The oncologist sighs deeply. Her eyes tell me we'll be getting to know each other very well.

"Well, I'm not going to sugarcoat it. It's not good," the doc says. "The cancer has spread. Your lymph nodes are affected. It's at least stage three."

I stare straight ahead. A lump appears in my throat that sticks like unchewed steak. My heart races. I try to look at the doctor but don't see her. Instead, I'm staring into the rest of my life, and, at this moment, it seems like a short life. I wonder what's next.

How hard will this be? Will I be sick? Will I . . . die?

The other three people in the room take turns telling me things. They indeed confirm and then repeatedly use the cuss word I was most afraid I would hear, the one that starts with a "C" and ends with "oh, crap." I know it's not good when it takes three professionals to cuss me this bad, and one is a chaplain of all people! That's like saying, "Hey, this ain't gonna go well, but here's a Gideon's Bible. Thanks for stopping by."

Other than these three scary folks, I am alone. I've never felt so alone in my life. Their words are the last thing I want to hear. No matter how hard I try to filter them out, they come through loud and clear.

As they continue talking, they give me statistics. They give me options. They speak about surgery. They throw words at me I've never heard. They . . .

Well, they might as well be singing Lynyrd Skynyrd's greatest hits because I don't hear anything after the first couple of minutes. To me, I've just been given a death sentence.

The word "cancer" has not been good to the people I love. I've lost many friends and family to it. And here I am, having the cuss word aimed right at me. Cuss words like "cancer" will make your allergies act a fool. Lately, mine have been so bad that I'm half dehydrated.

Life has taught me many cuss words that were hard to deal with. Scary words. Words with the ability to change people's lives. Words changed *my* life. Take the word "dementia" for example.

When the doctor uttered that bad word in the presence of my momma, we almost had to fist fight right there in his office. Little did I know that the journey we were about to embark upon would change her so much. I never realized how much it would change me.

I was there when many cuss words were spoken to my dad: lay-off, unemployment, heart attack. Dad took them all in stride. I think he was more upset when his auto mechanic uttered a double-cuss word: blown engine.

It was from my dad that I learned how to handle cuss words. I also learned how to use a few from him, but I watched how he handled the ones he had to face. He was the strongest man I have ever known. Nothing fazed him. He smiled no matter how bad his day was. Then, one day, I heard cuss words about him that broke me: "He's gone."

Those stung something awful. I wasn't prepared for those cuss words.

Then there was March 10, 2009. It was still early in the morning. My phone rang. My nephew was on the other end. You guessed it, more cuss words. "Something is wrong with Mom. Paramedics are on the way."

A few moments later, really bad cuss words. She too was gone. My sister had run to Jesus.

I told you; my life has been full of more cuss words than a Samuel L. Jackson movie.

"Your brother is slipping away." Those cuss words came as I gripped his hand tighter. I talked to him as he left this world. I don't even remember what all I told him, but I bet no cuss words were involved.

"Your son has a very large tumor on his liver." Those are the cuss words that taught me to pray on an entirely different level. I bawled like I'd been bobbing for onions in salt water when I prayed to God to fix him.

I begged, "I'll take it, God! Remove this pain and suffering from him and give it to me."

Have you ever felt like you were praying for the life of your child? You feel like you're the only one in the world on the party line with God. I have never switched back to praying like I did before that.

That's where I am at this moment. I am stunned, shocked, and ready to do the one thing I always do when cuss words come my way. I pray.

After my appointment, I sit in my truck for what seems like eternity. I call my wife. "It's not that bad," I tell her.

I try to never lie to her, but news like this does not get shared over the phone. I want to tell her face to face, so the cuss word can be followed by an embrace.

Then, I speak to God the entire hour it takes to drive myself home. I know I'm about to embark upon the hardest battle of my entire life, and I need Him. Every time I get worked up, He assures me He'll be right here with me every step of the way. I feel His presence on this drive.

There are still a lot of uncertainties, but I know I'm not alone. I know that no matter what's ahead of me, it fails in comparison to what He can do.

I know I trust Him. I know He loves me. And I know that God is bigger than this cancer.

CHAPTER 6

EVICTION DAY

It's surgery day! We've drawn an early kickoff time in this tournament of body part evictions, so here we're at 4:00 AM. Early starts like this usually mean we arrive, wait until lunch, and then proceed to the checkout where we sign over any belongings, children, and assets we have.

I enter the part of the building I'm told to, sign in, and get directed to another room where I'm told they'll call my name when it's my turn under the pocketknife. The room I wind up in is full of what seems like emphysema and lung transplant patients. A symphony of coughing, hacking, and wheezing greets us the moment we enter. Kristy reaches into her purse and pulls out an industrial size antibacterial hand dispenser and starts working it like a gambling addict hitting up a slot machine.

This room is much like all the other hospital waiting rooms I've spent time in—quite possibly the most boring room on the planet. They're all pretty much the same no matter where you go. A few books, the usual half-empty box of generic facial tissues, and a variety of well-thumbed-through magazines are scattered about. There are a few pieces of rather uninspired artwork on the beige-toned walls, some worn-out seating, and an end table covered with medical information pamphlets.

The large plant in the corner by the door is made of plastic and dust. A muted TV bolted to the wall plays drug advertisements on repeat. The citizens of this room glance up each time the door opens and then down again when their name is not called. We all look like slow motion bobble head dolls. We ache with hope that a nurse or other hospital official, or even the waiting room mayor, will call our name and take us to the nether regions of the hospital, or at least let us learn treasured information about a loved one's condition and location.

As a nurse walks past us, we get to hear the delightful music of squeaky soles on the tile floor. It complements the endless beeps from unseen machines and intercom announcements. The telephone on the receptionist's desk is lit up like a Christmas tree, but the calls are never answered.

I double-check all the information entered onto my patient information forms as the minutes add up and then go past the time I was instructed to arrive. I've signed my name where highlighted, check marked boxes where indicated, but what have I really signed? Am I absolving them in the unlikely event of my death as well as signing up for endless and automatic monthly payments?

A few people wander about the confines of the room. Some venture out in search of coffee or nourishment from vending machines, located in the next room, which were last serviced sometime during the Nixon administration. A few lucky ones are reunited with relatives thought lost to the giant medical machine. A child lay back in her father's arms, gently snoring after her hour-long cries for her mom.

An hour into my confinement, I work up the courage to venture toward the door to search for the restroom. Just then, a nurse walks in with a brightly colored and highly suspect clipboard.

Will my name be the next to be called? What information is really written on all those papers? I'm beginning to think they're some sort of betting pool, and the hospital staff watching us through the security cameras are selling chances on which one of us goes insane first.

Since my number is not up, I find the small restroom, holding my breath against the antiseptic spray set to overdrive and then exit as quickly as possible. I briskly amble back to the waiting room, hoping I haven't missed my appointment. Nothing has changed, except the commercial on the TV switched from high blood pressure medicine to asthma control inhalers. The movie trailer for this is better than the movie itself.

I settle back into my floral print chair and adjust the lumps in the cushion for comfort. The chemical smell from the custodian mopping the floor makes my nose itch. I reach for the most recent *Reader's Digest*. March 1998. I'm delighted to see that nobody has yet to fill out the vocabulary quiz.

The clipboard-wielding nurse ventures past and makes mysterious marks on the paper, no doubt checking off the losing entries of the lottery and says for perhaps the hundredth time since my arrival, "Only a few more minutes."

As those minutes turn into another hour and my butt begins to chafe from the constant shifting of positions, I realize that I feel all alone in the neutral-colored jail cell. My mouth is horribly dry because I was instructed not to eat or drink anything for the last month and a half it seems, and now my spit has turned into sludge that could be used as paint stripper.

Finally, I hear my name.

Before she can change her mind, I scramble to gather my items to follow the nurse. I hand her the patient forms and answer rapid-fire questions about illegal drug use, my date of birth, and whether I could be potentially pregnant. She's all business and moves like a feral cat when you turn the porch light on. I duck into the exam room mere inches before she slams the door shut.

I've been told to change into a fashionable gown designed out of facial tissues. Is this why every box in the waiting room was half full? I settle on the exam table just as a discreet knock precedes the abrupt entrance of another member of the hospital staff. Her motions seem rehearsed, as if her only intentions are to make it through her shift.

I try to position myself as instructed while she adjusts a robotic-looking machine and gathers items from a supply cabinet. She's apparently displeased with my efforts and then pushes, pulls, and twists me into what feels like the exact same position I placed myself into. I think this woman is a former Russian Olympic wrestler!

She leaves the room with the parting words, "Try to relax."

I close my eyes and try to figure out how to breathe, keep myself covered, and not move all at the same time. I wonder how long I'll be stuck like this only to hear, "O-kay, we are all done. Pay at the gate. Have a nice day!"

OVER THE NEXT HOUR, I have what seems like the entire population of Birmingham come in to introduce themselves and go over last-minute game plans. I feel like they're trying to talk me out of things.

At last, a member of the surgical team comes to wheel me away. By this point, I've already been given an intravenous drug to make me comfortable, so I'm talkative. Real talkative.

"So, you do understand everything we're doing, correct?" he asks.

"Boob job!" I shout rather excitedly.

He laughs. "We may squeeze that in."

The truth of the matter is I know the plan *exactly*. It scares the stew out of me.

They're going to slice a fairly large section off my rear end, flip me over like a side of beef, go in from the front, and take out the affected lymph nodes. It will take a few hours and a smoke break for the surgeon, but I should be in recovery by the evening news.

Down a series of turns and double doors, I reach the area where only card-carrying members are allowed. I say my goodbyes to Kristy and the kids before they disappear as the doors close. I watch them as the double doors become smaller until I can no longer see them.

For a brief moment, I wonder to myself if it will be the last time I'll ever see them. It feels scary. So very scary. Although it seems like there are a hundred medical personnel around me, I feel alone.

My mind drifts off again, this time not just to my own fragility but the fragility of the very ones depending on me. What will they do if they lose me? I'm their rock, their fan, their provider. I am always strong for them, often hiding what's really going on.

I'm reminded of the need to see them for who they are, to ask how they're truly doing, and to share the love of Jesus with them. But is it all too late? Have I done enough if this is really *it*?

I begin praying as I'm carted into the surgical room. Everything is so bright and painted white. They push my hospital bed next to a surgical gurney and instruct me to slide over to the next bed. Between instructions, I continue to pray my thoughts out to God.

Jesus tells us in **Mark 9:17-19 (NIV)**:

> *"A man in the crowd answered, 'Teacher, I*
> *brought you my son, who is possessed by a spirit*
> *that has robbed him of speech. Whenever it*
> *seizes him, it throws him to the ground. He*
> *foams at the mouth, gnashes his teeth, and*
> *becomes rigid. I asked your disciples to drive*
> *out the spirit, but they could not.' 'You*
> *unbelieving generation,' Jesus replied, 'how*
> *long shall I stay with you? How long shall I put*
> *up with you? Bring the boy to me.'"*

Like the father in the above Scripture, we must bring the subject before Jesus in faith, believing He can do anything but fail. So then, as I say a prayer for the surgery to go well, I need to learn to put the entire situation in God's hands, trusting that He knows what is best for the entire situation.

That's how I end my prayer. "Jesus, I trust You."

The anesthesiologist hooks another line into my IV. "Okay, here comes the good stuff," he says. "Count back from ten for me."

Ten, nine . . . eight . . . seven—

Lights out!

I'M STILL numb from the procedure when I wake. I'm groggy and slightly nauseated. There's pressure in my groin area but not pain. The area just above the bend of my leg—where doctors went in to retrieve the lymph nodes—feels like it has a thirty-pound weight lying on it.

Kristy has been escorted to me. She stands by my bed, holding my hand. Her smile makes me smile back. I'm as doped up as a crack addict in an alley, but I'm grinning like a possum. If I had to choose just one thing to see after waking up from surgery, it would always be her.

I notice how hot and humid it is, and I feel a stinging sensation all over my body; like sweat on a cut. I try to move, but my body feels stiff. The heat and I never get along. My mind is fuzzy at first, but I start remembering things.

I'm in a hospital. Why is it so hot? Aren't hospitals supposed to be cold?

My tongue is dried up and stuck to the roof of my mouth, and I can't swallow. I look at the table next to me and see a pitcher, hoping there's water in it. Kristy pours a drink for me into a small Styrofoam cup. I struggle a bit and sluggishly test my grip, touching each finger to my palm before grasping the cup and taking a drink. It's just a few sips, but wetting my mouth is amazing.

Things are working all right, so I attempt to sit up. It's a slow, painful process, but I get there eventually. I reach over to the pitcher and thankfully, there's more water in it. I drink it up. It tastes kind of stale. Better than nothing, but I definitely need more.

I place my feet on the ground and feel my muscles are working, but I'm just so weak and tired. I'm unsure if it's from the surgery; maybe a reaction from anesthesia? Maybe it's just the heat.

I stand, balancing myself with the side of the bed. I have no idea why I "need" to stand, but I have something to prove to myself. It's brief. I sit back on the bed, letting my mind swim through everything I've taken in.

Where is the doc? Is he going to talk to me? Did they get all the cancer? How long was I out?

I look around and see that there's a bag of my clothing and other belongings. I plead with Kristy to let me get dressed.

"Hey, champ," the surgeon says as he enters the room. "Everything went well. We had to cut out more than we thought, so you will be quite sore for a while, but we're confident we got it all."

"Thanks, Doc," I mumble. "When can I go back to work?"

"Let's focus on recovery first," he replies with a laugh. "It will be at least after lunch today."

He leaves without any other information. I'm still too confused to ask any questions. So instead, I just lie here, my mind racing.

I know our journey is just beginning. I know treatments will follow. I know we have a battle. Perhaps a war! But as I lie here regaining awareness, I know I trust a God that's already working on my behalf for the good of this situation.

I will have weak moments. I'm only human. But I know that in those weak moments, He will be teaching me, growing my faith, and showing me things to which I've been blind.

I still don't know how any of this can glorify God, but I don't have to. All I need to do is continue to trust that He will use this cancer for His glory. I need to trust that He will use me, in whatever capacity He needs, to do His work.

This is only the beginning, but I already know I am all in! This will be *His* story, not mine!

CHAPTER 7

SMILE, GOD LOVES YOU

Before you get too comfortable in your La-Z-Boy, on your mattress, or in your Buick, I have to tell you something very important: This chapter is written just for you.

When I decided to dive into what my battle looks like, I also thought about you. I thought about your illnesses, your mountains. I pondered what it's like to go through depression, financial hardships, and your refrigerator going out while you're on vacation. Bologna is costly these days. We're not even going to talk about how emotional we get when our bacon spoils.

No matter what you're going through, what you're healing from, or what the I.R.S. is claiming, I hope this chapter helps with your healing process.

Healing is a personal journey for each of us. The very fact that we have to heal from something means we've been injured. Emotionally, physically, mentally, spiritually—we experience pain in all these aspects of who we are as humans. Therefore, depending on our situations, we can be on very different paths to healing. Where some heal quickly, others might take their entire adult lives to heal from the crash that took Dale Earnhardt from us.

At this point in this book, I'm healing from my first surgery. That doesn't make my healing process any more difficult than yours.

We are all uniquely different, and our battles are important. Wherever you're at and whatever you've experienced, your feelings are valid. Your hurt is *real,* and you deserve to be loved and cared for by those around you.

I'VE NEVER BEEN SO uncomfortable in my life as I am the first day home after surgery. A twelve-inch scar runs from my back down to my money-maker. On my flip side is another scar where lymph nodes in my groin were removed. Needless to say, I am uncomfortable!

I could try positioning myself on either of my sides to avoid laying on the surgical scars, but watching Andy Griffith in such a way without getting a stiff neck is hard.

The Andy Griffith Show has always been a big part of my healing process. From pneumonia to broken bones, Andy and Barney could always make me feel better. I can't remember the first time I watched the show, but I do know I've been hooked ever since.

Nothing gives me as much "pure" joy as this incredibly special show. No show has ever been able to touch my heart as often or as deeply as the town of Mayberry and its "Aww, shucks" way of life nor has any show ever meant as much to me. It was something me and my old man shared together. It's even become a part of my vocabulary when I talk to others, as I often quote lines from episodes.

Sometimes, I encounter people who, upon finding out my love for all things Mayberry, will say to me, "Boy, I used to love watching that show."

I always reply, "Used to?!"

It's amazing to me how many people say they love the show but never watch it. I'm not trying to be critical, but when someone tells me they "love" and "used to" watch *The Andy Griffith Show,* I deduce that maybe they aren't as big of a nut as I am about the show. You see, the

Bible says that a merry heart will do you good just like medicine. I'm getting a little older each day, and I need my daily dose of medicine.

I recently finished reading Betty Lynn's autobiography, *Becoming Thelma Lou*. In her book, she pointed out how after a day of work and activity (for some, work is activity), people look forward to what helps them unwind and relax, and that's putting a little Mayberry into their lives at bedtime.

If she wasn't already in Heaven, I would ask the Queen of Mayberry if she'd been peeping in my windows because she described me to a "T." Nothing puts me in the frame of mind for rest and causes me to leave behind the concerns of the day like watching Barney tell Andy, "It's therapetic!" or hearing Andy tell Goober, "Why don't you have Floyd look at your eye? He's a barber."

So, here we are, the afternoon of Day One At Home . . . and I have to get out.

I figure the best antidote to get me going is sunshine. I pause Andy in the middle of him telling Otis to lock up after he sleeps off his self-induced sentence, step on to my back patio, and venture out into the backyard. It's still spring, but the temperature today makes it feel more like July.

The spring season is a time of new beginnings, when plants start to grow and flowers begin to bloom. My yard is evidence of such. I have to cut my grass, but I know the pollen will swell me up like I work on a shrimp boat with shellfish allergies.

Spring is also a time of cleaning; people often take advantage of the warmer weather to do some much-needed organizing and decluttering. For many, spring is a time of hope, as the days begin to grow longer and the weather gets nicer. It's a time to start fresh and set new goals. This surgery happened just in the season I need it to. I need hope and a fresh start.

I feel my scars stretch as I walk. My muscles are still groggy, and each step seems choreographed. Laughing at Andy and Barney didn't hurt near this bad, but I know walking will help my healing, both physically and emotionally.

The sun shining on me feels wonderful. I want to just sit out here for hours and reflect on how beautiful each day is. Even knowing what's waiting on me should God choose to call me home; I don't want to be taken from *this*. Here . . . It is all so wonderful.

As I continue my walk, I take out my phone and snap a picture of myself. A smile sits on my face so big that I can count my molars. I post it to my Facebook page, along with the caption *"Life is wonderful and cancer will not steal my smile."*

I then spend the next few minutes trying to respond to the many people who reach out to me, the people that love me and the ones I love. I don't care how much time it takes; I will never get tired of communicating with friends.

━━━⌈◦∞◦⌉━━━

OVER THE COURSE of the next two weeks, my body regains strength. I increase the length of my walks, and I'm slowly being weaned off the healing powers of *The Andy Griffith Show*. My appetite still hasn't found its way back, but my lack of exercise doesn't call for many calories anyway, so I'm not too worried.

I haven't been very active on social media, and I've received a few messages from folks who follow me asking how I am. They know I must be feeling bad when I don't write stories, blogs, and horrible episodes of grammar. I have, however, posted a few pictures from my daily walks, of which I included a smile with most.

"How can you be so happy going through all this?" one message asks. "You are always smiling."

Well, it's like my good friend, Buddy the Elf says, "Smiling is my favorite."

Everyone knows how to smile. It's one of the greatest gifts God gave us. A smile makes people feel good, and people look so beautiful when they smile.

When the joy in your life is obvious, it rubs off on others, but when you keep God's joy locked inside you and don't allow it to show on your face, you deprive those around you of a pleasant and refreshing experience.

Most people really don't understand how expressing joy will change their circumstances and, perhaps, the lives of others. Living your life with the joy of the Lord will chase off negative, depressing circumstances.

These scars I'm now making payments on are not fun, but smiling makes it better because I can say, "Guess what, cancer?! You can't steal my smile!"

I never would have thought that smiling was such a serious matter, but God spent several months trying to get this point across to me. Expressing joy through the calm delight of smiling brings good things into your life and shares the joy and light of the Lord with others.

Many see smiling simply as an involuntary response to things that bring you joy or inspire laughter. While this is certainly true, it overlooks an important point: Smiling can be a conscious, intentional choice. Whether your smile is genuine or not, it can act on your body and mind in a variety of positive ways, offering benefits for your health, your mood, and even the moods of people around you. Smiling makes people wonder what you're up to, and that's just plain fun.

In these first two weeks after surgery, smiling has been a forced emotion. I do more squinting and thinking than smiling. I look like a confused coonhound, and smiling is something I have to remind myself to do. After all, I'm still new to all the terminology; I'm learning words that are too big for me to afford, but I've been studying up on this new cancer treatment I'll be undergoing.

Prior to my surgery, a treatment called "immunotherapy" was picked up by major insurance companies. Doctors say I'm a candidate and I can get approval easily.

But what is immunotherapy? Two months ago, I had never heard of it.

As I've figured out, many of my friends haven't either. When I tell people it will take at least one year for me to finish my treatments for cancer, they're puzzled.

Immunotherapy is fairly new, and we're still learning all the side effects and gathering statistical information. Most people are more aware of *chemotherapy,* where strong doses are given in a short amount of time to attack the cancer. The downside is it also attacks everything else.

With *immunotherapy*, the chemo dose is lower and other drugs—in my case, Keytruda—will be used to go to battle, but winning the war takes longer. It's supposed to be better on our bodies. Immunotherapy is so powerful because it doesn't directly fight cancer. Instead, it prompts the patient's own immune system to recognize and then destroy cancer cells.

Once those drugs are coursing through me, my immune system will do the hard work. Of course, there are potential complications, or side effects . . .

My combination treatments will be given through a PowerPort surgically placed in my chest. Imagine wearing half a golf ball under your skin and trying to function normally. If I lift anything that causes my chest muscle to contract, it will pull as if it is coming out of my chest muscle. If I bump something against it, it will stab me. In a nutshell, I'll have to be careful but it's vital for my treatments.

I'll be exhausted afterward; good for nothing but lying on the couch, staring at the TV, and writing awful commentaries—but that's okay. I won't know what side effects will hit me after each treatment. It seems this drug picks and chooses what arsenal it will use each time.

Sometimes, treatments can cause the skin over the entire body to burn as if you have a sunburn. Your skin also becomes itchy. Other times, growing nausea hits at random, keeping you from eating much. Some treatments may come with hardly any side effects other than fatigue. Then, the very next treatment may be the one that rocks your world.

You're advised to rest and sleep as much as possible. Absolutely no stressful situations. Yeah. Okay! Have you seen the world we live in?

Immunotherapy is kinda like being in a boat and rowing against the tide, but if you keep rowing, if you don't give up, doctors are confident it will take you to calmer waters and maybe even land.

Because immunotherapy is so new—and combination treatment is even newer—predicting the side effects for an individual patient is not easy. Despite the battle that comes with it, I still have hope that I will be cured. I have given it *all* to God, and I know He will use it to His glory.

If I can use my testimony to lead others to Him, I'll take whatever comes.

I know it all sounds like a late-night horror show. It's enough to scare the stew out of me. Still, I've already made up my mind. I'm never giving up. I'm never gonna let cancer get the best of me, and I'll always smile.

THE FIRST DAY of treatment comes, and my anxiety is through the roof.

Kristy has been by my side every moment since the first cuss words were hollered at me, and as true as the Word of God, she's here on this day as well.

Walking into the UAB O'Neil Cancer Center is like starting my first day of an indefinite jail sentence. Even though I've read enough articles to kill my laptop, I still feel like I know very little about cancer treatments. I've watched videos, talked to survivors, and read books yet I feel about as educated on the subject as I am with Egyptian hieroglyphs. I come in smiling, though.

The nurse administering my pre-exam is nicer than a Presbyterian MeeMaw. She engages in talk with me on every subject except cancer.

"So, you're an author I hear," she states.

"Yes, ma'am!" *But please don't hold that against me.*

"What do you write?"

"Books," I reply.

She laughs. "No, silly! What genre?"

"Oh. Well, most of mine are in the Non-Grammar," I tell her.

"You mean nonfiction?" she asks.

"No."

We talk more about books, favorite authors, and kids. She asks about my hometown. Talk turns to our favorite football teams. I tell her mine is the Crimson Tide of Alabama, and she replies, "War Eagle!" I tell her I'll pray for her salvation, but she lets me know she's already found it 160 miles east of Tuscaloosa.

Then I notice something—a small silicone band around her name tag pinned to her scrubs. On it are the words **"God Is Bigger."**

It stops me dead in my tracks and pauses my "Roll Tide" antics. I think back to the first piece I wrote after learning I have cancer. It contained those very words! At the time, I didn't know how to finish it.

God is bigger than what? I remember asking myself.

Seeing that little band triggers something inside of me. I've seen one just like it. Back in 2012, a friend of mine gave me a band exactly like the one around the nurse's tag. He told me it was for a friend of his. Her name was Rachel.

Rachel Shaneyfelt was diagnosed with mesothelioma, a rare asbestos-related cancer and given only nine months to live. Can you imagine being told such a thing? I remember talking to my buddy as tears developed in his eyes.

"She's gonna beat this," he told me, "and she's gonna leave a mark in this world doing so."

While working as a nurse practitioner, Rachel was scheduled for a lung biopsy that never happened. The lesion had reduced in size.

She later told a doctor, "You're not going to believe this, but my lesion has shrunk 70 percent. Praise God!"

The atheist doctor said, "That's great, get yourself a T-shirt."

Rachel did. She bought 130 "God Is Bigger" T-shirts and gave them to nurses and staff.

In order to continue spreading the Word, Rachel purchased her very first batch of "God Is Bigger" bracelets, designed to draw attention to the solution, not the problem. She challenged her small group to take them and give them away to total strangers. In one week, the bracelets were gone. Within months, the demand went global. In 2014, because she couldn't continue paying for the bracelets, she started distributing apparel for a donation. Since then, the God Is Bigger Movement has distributed over 700,000 bracelets worldwide.

Rachel Shaneyfelt went home to be with her Savior on August 26, 2017. She will forever be missed by the thousands she impacted.

Rachel was a strong, courageous woman, and a huge inspiration to so many. And now, although I never met her, she's an inspiration in my young cancer journey. Seeing that band on that nametag instantly makes the corners of my mouth turn up into one of the biggest smiles I've ever produced.

"Where did you get that band?" I ask.

"Downstairs," she says, "in our treatment facility. You want one? I think we have a few left."

"Absolutely!" I holler.

"I'll call them and have you one waiting."

Sure enough, once I arrive in the treatment facility, I'm met with my bracelet and enough smiles to light up a Walmart parking lot during a snowstorm. I know the routine. I smile back. They're nicer to you when you speak their language.

They cart me in and give me the pick of the litter in treatment chairs. I choose one with a window view. From here I can see tall pines, the nearby interstate, and a Buick getting repoed.

Because I haven't had my PowerPort placed in my chest yet, I begin my immunotherapy loser-leave-town match through an intravenous needle in my arm. The "needle nurse" assures me I won't feel a thing. I should note at this point that the "needle nurse" is a compulsive liar and takes joy in seeing grown men squirm and whine like an injured Beagle.

I sit in a heated chair with an option to have my hindquarters massaged. I turn the setting to high. Kristy holds my hand until it turns blue. We talk. We don't say much about the "what-ifs" or the long road ahead of us. Instead, we talk about all the things God has allowed us to do over the years.

We talk about how, at one time, my faith was a baby, learning how to pray and believe in His grace. God was good to me. He was good to us. We talk about *those* things.

Before I know it, I've taken the first of many treatments . . . and I'm at peace.

AFTER TWO HOURS, three copays, and two boo-boo stickers on my shirt, I'm ready to go home and let the effects of my very first treatment kick in. I've heard the horror stories, so I'm prepared to be in bed for the next few days. I have every *Andy Griffith Show* highlighted on our channel lineup. There's an assortment of books already on my nightstand, and I saved a show on Netflix to watch later about the aliens living under Denver's airport. I am set.

As it turns out, it's not as bad as I've been told.

It's worse!

My body has gone into survival mode and is attacking everything that doesn't belong in it. I hurt all over. My muscles cramp as if I've run a marathon in a sweatsuit. My head hurts like I've been in a head-butting contest with a full-grown mountain ram. My appetite is that of any college kid in a frat house at 7:00 AM. on a Sunday. If I eat it, it will escape a few moments later.

I have to get up, and I have to get out. Breathing outside air will cure Ebola. It's amazing what the sunshine can do. You could be down one lung and running a fever of 220° but walk outside and breathe the air while the sun warms your face, and you'll feel like you could dunk on Shaquille O'Neal.

Once outside, I begin walking and looking. The spring rain brought new life to my yard. Flowers are in bloom. Birds are courting. Wasps are sizing me up.

I sit under an umbrella by our pool and gaze at the blessings around me. God has proved that there is so much for me to be thankful for. It is beautiful just to sit and take in all the wonderful animals and plants that God created, each with its own meaningful detail. I am thankful for the lessons nature has taught me about generosity. There is so much to learn from the natural world about how to live a life based on relationships, abundance, and giving.

The beauty of His creations often takes a back seat to the busyness of our days. We have lists as long as our arms to complete before sunset. Chores take us away from "seeing" because we are "doing." This new chapter I've entered has forced me to slow down and notice some of the things to which I've been blind.

When we sit at the Lord's feet and put aside the clamor of each day, we shall see the beauty of God. Indeed, we will hear the song of nature and lift our hearts to join in the chorus. When we are truly grateful for what's around us, we hunger for His knowledge and open our eyes, genuinely thankful for His generosity.

I sit here, smiling like I've just been given the keys to '68 Camaro. What else can you do when, not long ago, you were given a cancer diagnosis but now, you're in the fight and know that the One who created it all is the very One who can deliver you?

"What are you smiling so big about?" Kristy asks, surprising me, as I was caught up in my own world.

"Everything," I answer.

"For someone that just had their first cancer treatment, you sure seem happy," she says.

"I don't even know why I'm smiling," I say, turning to her. "I guess my heart told me to."

"Huh?"

"My heart is so happy," I continue. "God has been good to me. I know He's going to use this for more than I could ever imagine He could. I don't even know how, but I trust Him. My heart trusts Him. I guess I'm smiling from my heart."

I can't take credit for this heart smiling thing. It's been around since false teeth were invented.

One of my momma's favorite sayings was, "My heart is happy." She used to tell me that true happiness lives in our hearts and has nothing to do with bank accounts, cable TV, or dining establishments. "All that stuff is temporary. It makes our brains happy," she would say. "But God lets the stuff that really makes you happy live in your heart."

Dementia eventually took her from the world. When the disease hit, it moved fast. Pretty soon, she couldn't read her Bible, so I sat and read it to her. She smiled every time. The last time I read it to her, she held my hand. She mouthed the words to me.

"My heart is happy," she whispered.

She was smiling with her heart that day, much like I'm doing these first few days into my cancer battle.

Smile with your heart . . . I still think of her when I say that.

Truthfully, I thought it was pretty dumb at first. I didn't fully appreciate her words until I got older. I learned that smiles are deceptive. Smiles can give a false narrative.

They say smiling too much even means you're hiding something. Not Momma. She was an open book. Her heart was happy, and I knew it was real.

She used to tell me stories about life during the first few years of her marriage. "It was rough," she said.

They lived on dry beans and watered-down coffee. Dad earned pennies and spent nickels. The ends never met. But when Dad got home from work, they went for a walk every day.

They didn't seem too poor. They weren't hungry when they were together. They even felt like all the bills were paid. If they looked at the many things stacked up against them, they would have never been able to afford happiness. But they didn't look there. They looked at their hearts. They found that it was each other that created the biggest smiles, the ones that come from—you guessed it—the heart.

I remember the day I had to move her into a retirement home to get better treatment. There wasn't much to smile about that day. Each item we packed had a story. All stories come to an end, but I could tell in her face she wasn't ready for the ending.

She knew I was bothered. Even with dementia already taking a grip on her mind, she knew I was crying inside and out. She said, "Aww, don't miss me. I'm gonna have so much fun where I'm going."

She was lying, and we both knew it. We knew dementia was eating her alive. It kind of felt like my father was dying all over again, except this time, slowly.

Momma looked at me and said, "Smile."

I did because my momma told me to. It didn't come from the heart, though.

The thing is, I can't always smile, even though I wish I could. Life doesn't always seem fair. Smiles get buried so deep at times that it's hard for us to find them because being a human being is not easy.

Sometimes you worry. Sometimes you deal with hard issues. Sometimes you get overwhelmed. Sometimes you think too much. Sometimes you forget that your old heart needs rest from the heavy weight of life. Sometimes you frown.

More times than not, you fake it . . . and you smile. Even the fake ones make you feel better.

Maybe it tricks our minds. I'm easy to trick. I'm not that smart. I just know that smiling makes people think nothing is wrong, so they don't ask. And then, you don't have to talk about it. And *then*, you bury it all inside and you never have to worry about it again!

. . . Until you're sitting outside, under an umbrella by your pool, thanking God for all He's done for you. It's then that you find a *real* smile. One that comes from the heart.

Once you find that smile, you'll start realizing that you're already right in the thick of the healing process. That process starts with the attitude that healing *is* possible. Although you may not yet know all the "whys," you will start understanding the "hows."

God is how, and the smiles you're not willing to let go of are proof.

CHAPTER 8

THE COST OF LIVING

"Have you seen how much they charge for that treatment?" Kristy asks while looking through a stack of bills that could sink a bass boat. "This is crazy! How will we be able to pay for this? Why isn't the insurance paying more?"

It's been a couple of months since this ordeal began, and doctors are starting to get antsy about who's going to make their BMW payments. I meet my copays at each visit, but my insurance provider leaves a hefty amount of unpaid expenses for which I'm responsible. The amount shown on each bill is enough to make us want to return our last grocery pickup.

"We can live on Kool-Aid and Jolly Ranchers," I try to convince her.

The list price for each indicated dose of Keytruda immunotherapy, when given every three weeks, is $10,683.52.

Then there's the administrating doctor's fee, the lab fee, the oil change fee for the doctor's BMW, and finally, the office visit fee, which apparently is different from the doctor's fee.

By the time it's said and done, the cost of each appointment is over $12,000.00, and the doctor's car is good for another 3,000 miles.

My insurance company has agreed to pick up the bulk of this cost, but just the 20 percent left for me to pay is almost 2,500 big ones. Add the billed amount for the surgery, the anesthesiologist, the surgeon's tire rotation, and parking fees . . . Well, at this point, I owe the equivalent amount it would take to buy Guatemala. What I'm getting at is this—it costs a whole heaping lot to stay alive nowadays.

It hasn't always been like this. Growing up, we'd have pneumonia with a collapsed lung and our mommas fed us chicken soup and sent us to school. The cost of that was a whole country cheaper.

Don't get me wrong. I'm happy about the medical advancements of chicken soup, and I'm very grateful for insurance. I almost feel plum embarrassed that I have it so good. I even feel lucky at times.

I have an excellent oncologist and a large healthcare team on my side; I've responded in the most exceptional way possible to my first line of treatment (knock on wood); I have been able to access my treatment drugs—usually relatively easily—because of reasonable insurance, and I certainly have fewer barriers to care than those faced by many people without access to the treatment we have here in America.

I *know* it could be worse. I also know that when someone mentions the financial toxicity of cancer, we all too often go to the terrible stories of people with hundreds of thousands of dollars of medical debt that are fighting to hold on to their homes, cars, or their ability to continue to rack up more debt as they try to stay above dirt. It's horrendous, immoral, and infuriating.

So-called financial toxicity isn't always a massive kick to our untouchables. Sometimes, it is a way to let people show how much they love you. It's what I experience nearly every day. Without a support group, there's no way I would be able to retain my sanity.

Mental health is just as important as financial help. This was brought home to me during a recent conversation when the other person mentioned that regular mental health therapy should be considered a standard of care for people living with cancer. Of course, I too think it should be a standard of care.

If you search "mental health" on the American Society of Clinical Oncology's website, you find a lot of information about remaining positive during your battle. This indicates that it is an important part of cancer care, but it's one *you* must *choose* to pay for if you need ongoing, long-term mental health therapy. It's a standard of care* where the asterisk means "if you can afford it."

That's how it is for much of the care I receive, and I believe I'm not alone.

I'm "lucky" each visit with a specialist of any type is just fifty bucks. Each scan is a couple hundred bucks, whereas the total cost is in the thousands. Still . . .

When there are weeks where you have multiple visits, many scans, prescription costs, as well as other recovery needs, each dollar counts. Before you know it, you're a hundred grand in debt payable to the order of the cuss word.

In one moment, I've gone from a healthy person to a cancer patient. That's how long it takes for your entire life to change—*one* moment. The timing will turn out to have a devastating effect not only on my health; it will destroy me financially. That's what cancer does. It doesn't just affect one person. Instead, it changes entire families.

A lot of people are already in precarious financial positions before they even hear the word. It only takes one stroke of bad luck to wipe out what you have. I'm no different. I've saved and prepared for emergency situations, but rarely do emergency situations take everything in one withdrawal.

I start overthinking. I'm practically hyperventilating just thinking about being homeless and wearing a lawn bag for my winter coat. As fast as the bills come in, I just know that within three months, the home I have will be for sale. I'll have to choose between staying alive and the mortgage payment. I'm afraid I'll be in line at the food bank in the basement of a church within six months.

I feel like a complete failure, and it isn't even my fault. Cancer knocked on *my* door. I did not search it out.

What terrifies me more than anything is falling into a cycle of poverty. I read that it takes almost three generations—if not more—to get out of that cycle and that people who fall into depending on state and federal aid often remain in poverty because there's a chasm between making enough money to live and the types of jobs and income they can have based on their education.

I begin to accept that I cannot pay everything all at once. I know that as long as I'm attempting to pay, the hospital won't come after my truck, my home, or my vintage Atari game system. As the weeks pass, I accept that debt is a part of cancer. Financial instability is always a breath away. Accepting it and being happy about it are two different things, but letting God guide me and help me is enough to settle my nerves.

As I work through my treatments, I realize I'm not alone. I sit in treatment rooms with a lot of other working men and women who are on family medical leave or have lost their jobs because their treatment protocol is longer than the ninety days allowed by the Family Medical Leave Act. So, they're really worried. Like me, they've been working to support their families and have no resources. I'm fortunate in that my employer supports me 100 percent. I work when I feel like I'm able. I do what I can, and to them, it's enough.

I think to myself, *It's incredible that so many folks can get sick and find themselves in financial freefall because of it. No one asks to get sick.*

The unfairness of it all makes me angry. I haven't been this mad since *The Dukes of Hazzard* got canceled. So, I make a conscious decision: I will shift my thinking from "helpless" to "helping." I will help other people deal with their situations. I have no idea how, but God does. I just have to trust Him. After all, I told Him from the start that I am His to use during this whole mess.

Aside from the finances, I worry about what this will do to Kristy. She's a warrior, but she also hides a lot of things under her shell. I know she will be right by my side during my entire ordeal, but what will that do to her?

A cancer diagnosis will affect just about every aspect of a patient's life in some way. It can also have a practical impact, negatively affecting job security, finances, basic family dynamics, and more. It can all be very difficult to navigate and have a devastating emotional impact on the caregiving spouse or partner.

In most cases, couples draw closer during the cancer journey and come through the experience with their relationship intact. This is important because I truly believe being in a close relationship can dramatically improve patient outcomes. However, not all relationships are strong enough to survive a cancer diagnosis, and the details of the cancer course can make an impact as well.

Neglecting those around you can be easy when you're fighting for your life. Their needs do not go away because of what you're dealing with. Spouses tend to feel separation. Finances become something they fight over. The things once done together turn into things rarely done.

Although being in a close relationship during a cancer journey can improve outcomes, the stress of treatment and the diagnosis itself can take a toll on couples. This is where we have to be careful and draw close to the words of our vows. I'm blessed; Kristy has nurtured me and stayed by my side like I'm the winning lotto ticket, never letting me out of her sight.

A cancer diagnosis often has a ripple effect on how patients see themselves, on their lives, and on their relationships. When you think of it in the context of marriage, it brings additional pressure, distress, and changes to how a couple typically operates in terms of their relationship. In many cases, communication—which may have been difficult before the diagnosis—suffers. I get told all the time that I don't listen. I do, I just have a better filter than most guys.

I recall the first few hours after learning the news . . . I walked outside to be alone, and I wept until there were no tears left. It wasn't because of what lay ahead for me, but because I was thinking about what Kristy and the kids would go through. I knew worry, and possibly even depression, may find them.

Kristy automatically assumed the role of caregiver, doing all she can to help me, but not all partners are up for the job which can be physically and mentally grueling. Unable or unwilling to face the challenges, they simply walk away from the relationship. A variety of stressors may erupt as a couple works through cancer and recovery. One of the biggest stressors tends to be money—especially if finances were an issue prior to the cancer diagnosis. What may have been something they could manage before now becomes a much bigger issue and much harder to deal with.

Now all these bills have started coming in, so many at once that my mailbox nearly has a catastrophic engineering failure. We feel overwhelmed. There are questions upon questions—"How can we pay for all this? Will we lose our house?"—but we learn to pray and believe that God will see us through it. No matter what happens, it is in His will.

Tough times force us to ask some deep questions. Whether you believe in God or not, you've got to at least admit that you don't have all the answers. We need guidance and hope that are bigger than ourselves. I believe God would not enter me into something that would break me in every aspect, but I also wonder what I've done to tick God off.

Is it my lack of willpower against eating at buffets? Because I laughed at jokes unapproved by the Southern Baptist Association? I have no clue, but whatever I've done, I wish I hadn't. No matter what I've done, it's time for my faith to be tested. Perhaps that's been the goal the entire time.

Faith is essential at all times, but it's really important to rely on faith during difficult and trying times. Faith reminds us that God's in control and that we need to rely on Him to see us through, even when the path ahead is as dark and unsteady as a '74 Buick. He's steady, He's ready, and He's willing.

All of us are fighting fear these days. Maybe you feel buried by anxiety from the moment you open your eyes in the morning. Will my loved ones get sick? How will I make ends meet if I lose my job? Will the economy ever recover? Why does Netflix keep going up on their prices? Some of us entertain those thoughts and start to spiral, and others take the ostrich approach—burying their heads in the sand and waiting until it's over.

There's a third way to deal with fear, and it's the best one: Hand off your anxieties to God.

The first thing we need to get straight is this: God cares deeply about our suffering, and He invites us to cast our burdens on Him **(1 Peter 5:7)**.

Did you catch that?

God's not far away, kicking His feet up on some heavenly footstool, shaking his head, and hoping it works out for us. He's near to those who are broken and confused. He wants to take your anxiety from you. He wants to pay for your Netflix subscription.

Well, maybe not the last one, but you know what I mean. The question is, are you allowing Him to lift your burden?

Philippians 4:6-7 says you can trade your fears for God's peace if you're willing to lay out your requests to Him.

His peace is powerful! It's the only thing that will truly loosen your tight chest when you feel like you can't take another breath. Instead of white-knuckling your way through your anxiety and playing out millions of scenarios in your mind, let it go, lay your requests before God, and feel Him lift that heavy load off your back.

Take your worries to God. He's big enough to handle them.

There's an old-timey word that I want to introduce to you: *stewardship*. It basically means that you're entrusted to take care of something that belongs to someone else. Managing a team of people or resources at work is an example of stewardship because you've got someone to answer to.

Can you see where I'm headed with this? Yep—you're a steward of the money and resources that God's given you. Now, of course, you must take personal responsibility and work hard. In fact, because God has trusted you with a job, you better take it seriously! At the end of the day, your ability to earn money and build wealth is given to you by God, as seen in this verse:

"You may say to yourself, 'My power and the strength of my hands have produced this wealth for me.' But remember the LORD your God, for it is he who gives you the ability to produce wealth." (Deuteronomy 8:17-18 NIV)

You can trust God with the money He's given you because He's the real owner of everything under the sun! He's the ultimate source of our security.

As **1 Timothy 6:17 (NIV)** says, you shouldn't put your hope in wealth but instead:

> *"hope in God, who richly provides us with*
> *everything for our enjoyment."*

So, if God made and owns everything as **John 1:1-3** tells us, and He entrusts us as His stewards, that means we can depend on Him to provide. So, we have to ask ourselves whether we believe He is good . . . Will He take care of me? Are these hospital and medical bills going to keep causing my mailbox to fail?

In the book of Matthew, Jesus taught His followers through one of His most famous sermons:

"Therefore, I tell you, do not worry about your life . . . Look at the birds of the air; they do not sow or reap or store away in barns, and yet your heavenly Father feeds them. Are you not much more valuable than they?" **(Matthew 6:25-27 NIV)**

Look outside your window. Hopefully, you live in a place where you can see birds and hear them singing. They seem to be doing okay, don't they? Not a single one of those birds is watching in fear as the Dow plummets. None of them are stocking up on toilet paper and hand sanitizer.

I know this sounds ridiculous but hear me out. They're just birds! You're a human being who was carefully made in the divine image of God. Don't you think He cares more about you than the sparrows and the blue jays?

God isn't worried about supply chains and economic downturns. The pharmaceutical companies that could cure me but choose not to because their financial gain would be disrupted don't burden Him with anxiety. It isn't because He doesn't care but because none of it matters. God already has a plan! He feeds the birds day in and day out, and you better believe He'll take care of his children, too.

Have you ever heard the old joke, "You know why you'll never see a

U-Haul behind a hearse? Because you can't take your stuff with you when you go!"

It's tempting to work like crazy to keep up with the Joneses; piling up stuff and chasing down the next purchase, but the Bible warns us against the temptation to hoard our wealth. Instead, we're encouraged to be **"rich toward God." (Luke 12:21 NIV)**

This means that we must use everything in our lives (including our money) to honor Him.

Trusting God's provision leads to contentment—being grateful for what we have. This idea appears all over the Bible. Take this verse, for example:

"Naked I came from my mother's womb, and naked I will depart. The LORD gave and the LORD has taken away; may the name of the LORD be praised." **(Job 1:21 NIV)**

When you've placed your trust in God and what He provides, you're free to be content with what you have right now. It helps you loosen your grip on your assets. Contentment is an incredibly important habit to practice when times are good and when times are bad. Gratitude changes your perspective because it shifts your focus from what you don't have to what you do have.

I have learned the secret of being content in any and every situation, whether well-fed or hungry, whether living in plenty or in want. As **Philippians 4:12-13** tells me, I can do *all* this through Him who gives me strength.

A relationship with God sets you free from worry and comparison. You just take it one day at a time. In times of abundance and crisis, contentment is the key to experiencing joy and gratitude.

This is where it gets fun. If you're applying some of these principles, you'll be free to enjoy your money without being controlled by it. You'll also recognize God's outrageous generosity more and more, and you'll want to treat others the same way! Ultimately, you won't let the stress of not having money cause you to lose faith in what you'll do when the bills start piling up.

But I am starting to worry.

A few months into this battle, I can already see the effects on my family. We cut back on going out. There will be no vacation. Name-brand bologna is a thing of the past. Even our dogs are chewing generic dog food. One almost ran away and joined the stray union.

My cousin, Scott, wants to help. He knows things will be tough; he too is fighting ailments such as diabetes that cause a strain on his checkbook, but Scott is about as compassionate as Mother Teresa. His heart is bigger than his bankroll.

Scott knows cars, and he knows people. So, he calls people who like cars. A few texts are sent. Plans are made. Scott is going to hold a car show to help me pay off some bills! And it will be at the church I attend.

I FIGURE a few cars might show up, but when I arrive, I can't believe what I'm seeing. The parking lot is nearly full.

There are old cars. New cars. Big trucks and little trucks. Even a huge boom truck flying a flag the size of Walmart. There are cars with $10,000 paint jobs and rat rods with hardly any paint at all. Some lie flat on the ground and others I can almost walk under.

I've never seen a car that cost more than my house until now. A McLaren 720 sits in all its glory while I drool puddles around it. I want to sit in it but I'm afraid I'll never get back out. It's low, at least thirty feet below sea level.

Little kids point. They "ooh" and "ahh." They run and play in jump houses. Flavored icees have already stained their shirts. People throw axes and they aren't even mad. They ride mechanical bulls, eat desserts that cause catastrophic diabetes, and they all wear smiles.

Food trucks are lined up, filling the air with the scent of all things unapproved by the surgeon general. Cardiologists pace the lot, passing out their business cards. People mingle. They laugh. They smile so big their jaws will ache for days. They discuss important things—things like four-barrel carburetors and positive traction rear-ends.

Herds of gearheads gather under trees and tents. Chatter about new project builds and upcoming shows fill the air. A fella mentions his new paint job had "fisheyes" in it, referring to a paint blemish. Those listening remove their caps and have a moment of silence for their friend. One places a hand on his friend's shoulder, shakes his head, and wipes a tear before shuffling away.

Gearheads are awesome people. They're a tight-knit bunch. Almost like a motorcycle gang but with bigger bellies and blood pressure medication. They help one another. They care about what each other goes through, and they show up when someone organizes an event to help one of their own.

I have always loved these types of things. I've organized events like these for over two decades. It's not so much the event itself as it is the aftermath I love. Events like this have helped me raise thousands of dollars to help people in need. I've seen little kids light up because Santa showed up with armloads of toys. I've watched moms cry because power bills got paid. I have even witnessed big hairy men bawl like babies because they got a new pair of work boots—the first brand new pair they ever had.

I've held events with my giant-hearted buddies that paid rent, helped high school seniors pay fees, and delivered groceries to hungry families. Good things. No, these types of things are not just good; as the cereal tiger says, "They're great!" I've always enjoyed them.

But today, I don't know how to act. I'm not organizing this amazing event. Instead, it is for me.

I have doctors at cancer treatment facilities that need to retire by age fifty-five. I have surgeons trying to buy new BMWs. They send me bills too heavy to carry. Pharmaceutical companies are trying to build bigger facilities so they can send free medicine to foreign countries. To do that, they charge me $10,474.08 for each treatment I take, which will go on until next year, or until—

Well, it will continue for some time. Blue Cross Blue Shield said they'll cover some of the costs but not all. They want to retire, too, and build beach houses for their executives.

So, to make all those people happy, my hard-headed cousin Scott and a few of my knucklehead friends got together and put all this together. They want my mailbox to straighten back up. They want to help pay for those big houses and retirements. They're doing their best to make me as uncomfortable as a squirrel on a four-lane. It's working.

It's hard being on the other side of these events. I'm supposed to be the one running myself dehydrated, making sure everything goes off without a hitch. At this one, I awkwardly try to walk around and thank everyone, even though I know I can't.

I apologize. I'm tired. It's hot. I also got pretty sick, but I won't let anyone know right now. This is all for me, and I refuse to disappoint anyone by leaving.

See, this thing came from above. Sure, my cousin and my buddies put this shindig on, but God orchestrated it because I said those little words: *"I trust You."*

I hand a small wristband to everyone I talk to. It has a simple message on it but it's an important one. It's one that can be applied to whatever mountain your "cancer" may be. Maybe it's depression. Finances may be your mountain. It could be relationship issues. Maybe something at work is bringing you down. It might be health issues. Whatever it is, there's a message on that little band that will tell you all you need to know: *God is bigger!* So, I give them out like a politician handing out football schedules in an election year.

I see many people wearing shirts with a logo I designed a few years ago. It's a simple design: a cross with roots. It reminds me that our faith is rooted in Christ and what He has done for us. Around it are the words **"God Is Bigger."** Under it, **"Team Russell."**

I know it's bigger than that. All these people—the organizers, the donors, the people that came, the vendors—they're not just Team Russell. This is God's team. He sent *you*, too.

I smile all day. I'm witnessing the other side of what I've done for years. I finally know what it means for a car show to bring the community together and cause saltwater to leak down faces.

At the awards ceremony at the end of the day, I try to think of something to say to show my appreciation. Words don't seem to do justice. I really don't know how to put my feelings into words.

A news crew sticks a camera and mic in my face. They ask what it all means to me. I silently ask God to give me words and not make me sound stupid. As I peer into the camera, the only words I can think of are, "It means that God is bigger!"

⚬

COMPASSION AND FINANCES—THOSE words find each other often. They show up at your house when you get sick. Casseroles line your front porch like a culinary yard sale. That's what folks do when someone they love is in need. They feed them and hope it will help pull them from the depths of double pneumonia.

If you have kids, think back to a time when you had a special gift for them. Maybe you surprised them with a puppy on Christmas morning, or you finally bought them their first iPhone.

Most parents—even though not perfect—want to do their best and take care of their children. We find great joy in seeing their faces light up when they get something they've been asking for. And you know what? God has the same generous heart toward His children! He gives good things to those who ask for them, and He delights in our joy **(Matthew 7:9-12)**.

Generosity is contagious. When you've received something good, it's a natural response to overflow that goodness onto others. Being generous is a powerful antidote to fear because it forces you to get your focus off of your own needs. It forces you to put your money where your mouth is.

This is how we know what love is:

"Jesus Christ laid down his life for us. And we ought to lay down our lives for our brothers and sisters . . . Let us not love with words or speech but with actions and in truth." **(1 John 3:16-18 NIV)**

God notices when we give, and He's pleased by our generosity **(Matthew 6:2-4)**. If you're short on cash, that's okay. There are endless possibilities on how to be generous with your time, your talents, and your friendship.

Loss is painful. It's real. We cannot make sense of all the evil in the world. It's a very human response to ask, "Where's God in all this? Why doesn't He do something?"

If you want to know where God is in the midst of suffering, all you have to do is picture Jesus on the cross. If you're wondering why He doesn't do something, remember the work He accomplished to conquer death and bring us hope.

God is well acquainted with loss and pain. He took it upon himself to come to Earth and share in all the same brokenness we experience. Because of the mission He accomplished, we can place our trust in Him and have hope that He can heal our diseases and restore our fortunes.

Even in the darkest moments, God promises to deliver his people, protect them, and ultimately, prosper them. We can trust that He will do the same for us. There's only one way to financial peace, and that's walking daily with the Prince of Peace, Christ Jesus.

CHAPTER 9

YOU'VE GOT TO BE
KIDDING ME

After a few months of treatments, I've finally found my groove. These things aren't scary anymore. My treatment port has been placed, treatments are scheduled and received like clockwork, and I've accepted the fact that what I'm going through is my new normal.

Does it suck? Like a Dyson!

I hate the day after treatment. I have no energy and ache like an NFL linebacker took his dietary frustrations out on me. My wallet is thin, my days are long, and my sleep is nonexistent.

And it's about to get worse.

To fully understand what's happening at this point, I need to back up to the starting line.

WHEN I WAS FIRST DIAGNOSED with metastatic melanoma, I swallowed hard as my oncologist explained my rather limited options. I felt emptied of incentive. Devoid of purpose. I just wanted to be rid of the tumor.

Like a Southern Baptist deacon at a Metallica concert, I was as nervous. My first thoughts were like those of most people when they first hear that cuss word: anything but pleasant.

Within weeks, I underwent surgery and began my long recovery. I had no idea what I was getting into and sought no help in coping. Being an old-school male, I simply toughed it out. However, my silent struggle was not invisible to my wife, God help her soul. She was an angel through it all. She knew when I was having a bad day without me having to say anything.

I wasn't prepared for complications, like a ruptured port. I almost bled to death when that happened. Then there was another surgery to remove it. Then another to place a new port. I was getting cut on so much that the doctors contemplated adding a zipper.

Though I acted courageously, I was seething inside. At times, my anger overflowed by being short or silent with those around me, but it mostly feasted on me. I became depressed. I functioned, but I didn't engage with others or with life the way I once did.

I appeared happy, energetic, and even healthy because I was good at faking it. Inside, I felt like everything that could go wrong was and had. But, as I would soon find out, more can go wrong.

And it does.

AT MY FIFTH TREATMENT, my doctor informs me that there is something on my last PET scan that doesn't look right. Another tumor has been discovered, this time in my left kidney. The culprit? Renal cell carcinoma.

"Is this caused by the melanoma spreading?" I ask, clueless how any of this stuff works.

"Nope! Not at all," he replies. "You are that rare specimen who has developed a second primary cancer totally unrelated to the first."

Great! I think. *If I'm going to do it, let's do it big.*

We talk about options. Another surgery is unavoidable. This booger must come out. We could try to shrink it and save the kidney, but it's not guaranteed to work.

My immunotherapy doses will increase in strength, which doesn't sound like fun either. They're already kicking my hindquarters.

As I will soon find out, only 1 to 3 percent of cancer survivors develop a second cancer different from the originally treated cancer. In my case, the same drug, Keytruda, can fight the melanoma *and* renal cell carcinoma. If there's a silver lining, this is it. However, even thinking about the possibility of having a second cancer is stressful.

I decide to stand taller. If I'm ever going to be someone who hollers for God during a trial, this is my golden opportunity. I have a stage. I have a battle: not one but two types of cancer . . .

I also can't help but to think back once again to that December night and my prayer: *"Lord, do something big in my life that glorifies You."* Two types of cancer is pretty big!

God is doing things, but I'm still pondering what my end of the deal is. I know He will show me when I'm ready, but it seems there's nothing I can do to make things any better, and I definitely don't feel like I'm glorifying Him.

I have learned that there is no one way to respond to a cancer diagnosis. A range of choices challenges each one who hears the fateful words. At times, we become passive because the way forward seems too daunting. Other times, we may feel rage at fate for cursing us so. We may become frantic in searching for the one magic bullet that will make everything all right again.

The fact is that a cancer diagnosis reveals something about ourselves we might benefit from learning. The revelations vary. For me, it's the two-headed beast of anger and how to keep that beast engaged in a positive way, but it's about this stage when I start noticing something.

I've journaled and blogged and even published books for some time. Writing a "feel-good" story and posting it to social media is nothing new for me. However, the interaction from my readers now is beginning to *really* take off.

My followers grow by numbers I've never before witnessed. I'm receiving more and more messages from people I've never met. Some say my openness about my journey and relationship with Christ helped them. Others say it's rekindled a fire in their life to chase God.

The ultimate messages that come in saying that they've *found* Christ because of me . . . Wow! That alone is worth every treatment, every surgery, all the pain, and every debt this cancer has brought me and will bring me.

When I began sharing my initial cancer diagnosis with friends, more than one confessed in all caps, "I HATE CANCER!" I couldn't help but think, *Yeah, me too!* but I did my best to remain positive.

As I share the news of this second and unrelated cancer that's been found in me, my friends and family cuss the bad word like it slapped their momma. I get it. Nothing is lovable about cancer, nothing joyful about malignant tumors, and definitely nothing fun about surgery, treatments, constant pain, and all the rest that comes with this living hell.

What's happening is something that should have broken me. In a way, it has. In an even more powerful way, it's pushed me so hard toward Christ that I've almost knocked Him down coming through the door. So, there's another side to this unexpected journey. One I actually embrace.

Some glorious, eye-opening, wouldn't-trade-them-for-anything moments come once I'm willing to accept the battle and use it to glorify God!

"HOW CAN CANCER GLORIFY GOD?"

Glad you've asked.

You see, God gave me a new desire to worship Him. I have an undeniable need to tell as many people as I can about how Christ changed my life. In a way, I'm thankful for my battle.

"Thankful . . . Really?"

Absolutely!

"Give thanks in all circumstances; for this is God's will for you in Christ Jesus." **(1 Thessalonians 5:18 NIV)**

"Russell, have you lost your ever-loving mind? Are you saying you're grateful to have cancer?"

Yes, that's what I'm saying.

Feel free to shake your head, roll your eyes, or sigh loudly. What I'm about to share may sound like a guy who's swallowed one too many steroid pills before my latest chemical-induced treatment and is floating on a drug euphoria.

The truth is, my gratitude has nothing to do with chemicals and everything to do with Christ. After all the years of knowing Him as my Lord and Savior, I now know Him as my Comforter, Healer, and Friend. I have never been more aware of His presence or more in awe of His power. And I've never felt more compelled to speak His name or sing His praises!

Though I wouldn't wish cancer on anyone, I long for my brothers and sisters in Christ to experience firsthand what happens when we accept the reality of our circumstances and not only trust God but also thank Him for the path He has laid out for us.

There are many reasons to be thankful through a hard season. A greater sense of His faithfulness is right on top of those reasons.

When I cried out to Him from my hospital bed before my first surgery, He was already there, calming my broken heart, assuring me of His love, just as His Word tells us:

"Your love, LORD, reaches to the heavens, your faithfulness to the skies." **(Psalm 36:5 NIV)**

I have a richer understanding of His peace. After the oncologist explained my diagnosis, the Lord dried my tears and reminded me of

His sovereignty in all things. Since God's in charge and we are not, we can let go of our anxious thoughts and rest in Him, knowing this:

"And the peace of God, which transcends all understanding, will guard your hearts and your minds in Christ Jesus." **(Philippians 4:7 NIV)**

I have a constant assurance of His goodness. Because His plans for us are always good and always purposeful, I can lift my tired head and say:

"I remain confident of this: I will see the goodness of the **Lord** *in the land of the living."* **(Psalm 27:13).**

I have a deeper dependence on His presence. Desperately aware of my need for Jesus, I pray more often and more earnestly than ever before. When I'm on my knees, He meets me without fail. I am reminded that we should:

"Devote yourselves to prayer, being watchful and thankful." **(Colossians 4:2 NIV)**

I have a fresh experience of His freedom. Of all the emotions that have washed over me, fear held sway for only one terrible day. After much weeping and gnashing of teeth, by God's grace, I chose to stand on His truth and be set free:

"So do not fear, for I am with you; do not be dismayed, for I am your God." **(Isaiah 41:10 NIV)**

There's a clearer vision of His hope. Whatever the outcome—healing or Heaven—God holds out a bright beacon of hope for my future *and yours*, and He provides the greatest reason for gratitude:

"Therefore, since we are receiving a kingdom that cannot be shaken, let us be thankful . . ." **(Hebrews 12:28 NIV)**

Whatever you might be going through right now, I'm here to tell you that once you decide to use what was formed against you for His good, you'll feel peace like you've never known. I only wish I could explain it.

Am I thankful? I'm thankful cancer has already lost . . . because I have a God that comforts me.

I believe at this point in this journey, God is already using me *and* this cuss word for His glory. For that, I am extremely thankful.

This battle causes me to enjoy the little things. I make more time for friends. I realize how easily life can be ripped from us. He has shown me new things that I was blind to before.

God talks to me through His Word but also through circumstances. He is putting me in place to meet new people. Even in places that I escape to for peace of mind, He puts people in my path, like an old friend I reacquainted with not long ago.

I STOOD on the bank of the Black Warrior River in Tuscaloosa, Alabama. It was an overcast day, one perfect for getting a fishing line tangled in trees, but I hadn't brought my tackle box. I was there for another reason. I was reflecting on news that still hadn't fully sunk in.

Just days prior, I sat in a room with three professionals with enough letters after their names to make them look Russian. They were there to give me "the news." I was there to crumble into a heap and wonder why.

I spent two days pondering that question. They told me there would be more surgeries and treatments. They talked about increasing the dosage of the chemicals already being pumped into me, some so strong the nurses administering them have to wear special suits and face shields. I wasn't as scared of it all as I was worried about the uncertainty of things to come.

I'm not even sure what brought me to the banks of that muddy water. There's something about a flowing river and the waves crashing against red clay banks that helps clear your mind. At least, it does mine. So, I stared off into the heavens and talked to Momma, Dad, and God. I spoke like I could see them. Then I heard it.

"Russell?!"

My eyes widened. I held my breath. It was as if I could hear *Him* talking back to me.

"God?"

"Russell Estes?!"

"Yes! It's me, God! I'm right here!"

"Man, I haven't seen you in over ten years."

"But . . . but . . . I was at church last Sunday . . . "

The voice didn't sound as I had thought God would. I was a little worried He didn't recognize me. It was then I heard a noise behind me and turned to see an old friend standing there.

"Whatcha doing out here?" he asked. "You fishing?"

"Hey, man! Nah, just passing time. And you're right, been at least ten years," I answered after regaining awareness of where I was. "What brings you around? I heard you moved off to Chicago or somewhere that don't believe in sweet tea."

"Had to move back. Pop's health went in the wrong direction."

We talked for a good half hour. He told me about his dad and how cancer had changed everything.

"It's been a rough ride, but we are fighting it together," my friend said.

We also talked about my diagnosis and how doctors had tried scaring the bejeebers out of me with big words and long needles.

"It's nothing God can't handle," I told him, almost as if trying to reassure myself of what I already knew.

"Yeah, I know. It's just tough to see my old man like this."

My run-in with my buddy may have been coincidental, but as we talked, I found myself being more of the one consoling than the one who, just moments earlier, needed to hear something good. We exchanged numbers, agreed to pray for each other's needs, and went our separate ways.

A few weeks later, I thought about my friend. I texted him:

> "How's your dad? Been praying for him
> daily."

My phone rang within seconds.

"Hey, man. Sorry I didn't call you. It's just been a whirlwind the last couple of weeks. Pop passed away last week."

A lump developed in my throat. I tried to find the right words. I didn't have them.

My friend told me he had promised his dad all sorts of things and he was beating himself up for not getting around to them.

"He had a bucket list, man. Just simple stuff. I tried to knock off a few for him, but . . . Man, I just waited too long to start," he tells me through an emotional stutter. "The week before he passed, he wanted to go to Savannah. Said he'd never seen that coastline before. I thought he was too tired for the trip, so I talked him outta it. Man! I . . . I still . . ."

I could tell he was hurt. Again, I didn't know what to say. In a rare moment, I was at a loss for words.

As I sat there that evening, wondering about my own diagnosis and the road ahead of me, I realized I knew exactly what I should have said but did not.

The day before doctors pointed out my cancer and used words I had to look up, I had many plans for the upcoming summer—vacations, pool parties, weekend-long fishing trips—but everything changed the very next day. I realized that many of the things I wanted to do really didn't matter anymore. I found a new bucket list; one I should have been working on all along.

I called my buddy back up. I told him something that I didn't even have to rehearse:

"Hey listen, man; you wanna know what makes this ol' life worth a hill of beans? It ain't what you think. I bet there ain't a person in Heaven that would say, 'Dadgummit, I wish I woulda taken a cruise, went to Vegas, rode a bull, or done something really scary but brave.' And I bet if you lined them all up next to the pearly gates, they wouldn't give a double-cuss word about whether or not they seen the coastline off Savannah."

I was rambling, but I wasn't finished:

"You know what matters when you go through this stuff? You walk around all day, and you think about one thing, man. *One* thing. It ain't places or exotic foods . . . not even fast cars or big boats. You think about the people you love. You wish you could've spent more time with them before you were sick. It ain't about nothin' else. I don't have to travel to an island to check this stuff off. I can love my people anywhere!

"Maybe you wish you woulda kept up with old friends instead of losing touch. You hope you were there for your friends when they needed you. You wish you woulda worked less hours and stayed out late with your kids until the last lightning bug was caught. You think about how you could just hold your wife and kids for every hour of the day because you're too scared to let go. Look, man, you were *there* when your daddy needed you. You picked up your entire life and moved back here to be by his side when he needed you most. THAT! *That* is what matters!"

THE CONVERSATION that day was one I needed to hear as much as my friend. That chance encounter on the banks of a river was no chance. It was orchestrated by God Himself. It is just one of many examples of what my battle has opened my eyes to.

I have a good chance of beating this thing. Sure, there are scary thoughts that bounce around inside my head that say I may not, but a thousand times over, I think I will. I truly believe that.

I don't think I'll beat it for just a year . . . a couple of years . . . or even ten. I think I'll whoop this old cuss word and live to be too old to drive. But just in case it ain't in God's plan, I'm at peace with that, too. So, I better include a little more.

I ain't afraid of dying. I'm afraid I haven't told my people just how much I love them. That's my bucket list.

And so, over the next few months of a double-cuss word diagnosis, I amp up my God-game! I whoop and holler for Christ like one of the original disciples. Folks think I've gone mad, but I haven't. I've come to reason about all the "whys." I have a bunch of them!

See, my life was interrupted. I found myself asking, "Why, God? Why would You let this happen? Why would You allow this cancer to hold me back from the things I thought You wanted me to achieve?"

What I felt God say in response was that I simply needed to trust Him on this path. Yes, He could heal me, but would I trust Him even if He didn't?

That was a hard pill to swallow.

It took me a couple of weeks of wrestling with the concept, but after many tears and *Andy Griffith Show* episodes, I realized that my response was, "YES."

Yes, I can, and I will trust God, even if He doesn't take away my cancer.

The Bible says He is trustworthy, and I choose to believe it. I put my faith in Him because I know He won't be careless with me. I lean into a long-time favorite verse:

"Cast all your anxiety on him because he cares for you." **(1 Peter 5:7 NIV)**

So, I've decided to stop asking God to instantly fix me and instead trust Him through the process of treatment. What I found during my treatment is that although it is hard, God has woven blessings into this journey.

When I really thought I might die, the world became insanely beautiful. Reminded of my own mortality, I now drink in sights and sounds like I'll never see or hear them again. I step through my door in the morning, and I am struck by the sight of dew drops on leaves—the way the light filters in through branches, or the way flowers close up so tightly at night but open themselves wide to the sun during the day.

I get up every day excited to watch the sunrise. It's become something I write about often and share with my readers. The beauty around me has become so acute and intense that it almost hurts. Having my life threatened led me to a deeper appreciation of creation; I can see God's artistic hand everywhere.

I'm also blessed with a special closeness to Jesus. I'm surprised because I don't feel like walking with Him through this time is hard work; I feel like He actually carries me.

I'm generally a bit of a pessimist and prone to negativity, but it seems like Jesus is helping me to feel more positive and upbeat than normal. Yes, it's still challenging a lot of the time, but I always feel Him with me, and I have an unexpected peace deep in my heart.

Having cancer has also opened up some doors and given me a platform from which I can share more about God's love. I've been speaking at events and blogging, and that has not only helped me to process my experience, but it's also allowed me to speak life and hope to a wide array of people I wouldn't have otherwise met.

Do these good things mean that I think cancer is God's good plan? No. No way.

Revelation 21:4 tells us when He makes everything new, there will be no more sickness and weeping. Cancer was not God's plan for mankind, and it won't reign forever—He *will* put an end to it. Unfortunately, for now, it's here, and it affects roughly a third of people at some point in their lives.

As I continue my fight against cancer, I know God isn't sitting up in Heaven telling me to toughen up. He is right here *with* me, weeping *with* me at the brokenness of my body. I know because Jesus has compassion on His creation.

When Jesus's friend Lazarus died, Jesus wept at the destruction and sadness—even though He knew the story had a happy ending! He knew He would raise Lazarus from the dead, yet He was overcome to the point of weeping **(John 11:35)**. So, I know it hurts God to see His creation suffer and be cut up, poisoned, and irradiated. For now, though, I believe God can use even this horrible disease to do wonderful and surprising things.

While we may be shocked by a diagnosis of cancer, God is not. He already knows how He is going to bring about something beautiful from it. He's the one who replaces ashes with a crown of beauty and turns mourning into dancing **(Isaiah 61:3, Psalm 30:11)**.

This means we can stop fretting and trust Him with our lives. In fact, in **Matthew 6:25-27** and **Philippians 4:6-7**, He tells us we *must*.

I'm still fighting. I still struggle with my health, the ongoing side effects, and the anxiety of more cancer being found. However, I am so grateful for all the good God has done and will continue to do on this journey.

Cancer, sickness, or illness is not God's plan for you or any of His precious creations but trusting Him is. It takes time to fully trust all this because it is a lot, but it can be done through faith.

As the shock from *everything* that comes with cancer begins wearing off, God starts pouring out His love on us through His church. By the grace of God, we're able to put all the questions aside and rest in His goodness.

This is where our theology gets the ultimate test. Do we trust in His sovereignty, or is that just something we say when things don't make sense? I like to say that I will "rest in His sovereignty but reach for His promises."

Oh, the peace of knowing GOD IS SOVEREIGN! He knows all, sees all, is all, and He is not surprised by cancer.

Romans 11:36 (NIV) says,

*"For from Him and through Him and to Him are
all things. To Him be glory forever! Amen."*

ALL things means ALL things. If all things are from Him and through Him and to Him, that includes this cancer. We should stop asking "why" and begin to ask God to be glorified in our suffering.

I can't explain what happens in our hearts as we suffer. I can't even begin to fathom how God can be glorified in cancer, tears, sleepless nights, or treatments that make me feel horrible—but somehow, He is. In a million ways we may never know, He is.

So many lives are affected by our suffering. For example, the church is rallying around me like I've never seen. Families are so burdened by our struggle that it brings them to their knees, some for the first time in a long time. Friends, new and old, are drawing closer to Christ as I share my journey. There's a beauty in that which I can't explain: the beauty of suffering for Christ and taking part in His suffering.

God's way of showing us love has been redefined through this battle. I feel more loved because God makes so much of this journey to be *our* journey. At the cost of His Son, He enables us all to enjoy making much of Him forever. My happiness hangs on seeing the cross of Christ as a witness. God's glory in Christ is the foundation of gladness!

God making much of me shouldn't be the way I know He loves me. Having a nice American lifestyle, a house, or a car does not mean I'm "blessed." They certainly can be God's blessings, but so can Him asking us to suffer for His glory. In fact, the love you feel in suffering carries so much more weight.

James 1:2-4 (ESV) says,

> *"Count it all joy, my brothers, when you meet trials of various kinds, for you know that the testing of your faith produces steadfastness. And let steadfastness have its full effect, that you may be perfect and complete, lacking in nothing."*

Does that mean we can find joy in trials and suffering? Yes!

The joy of the Lord and my comfort have nothing to do with each other. My joy is found in His glory and in Him walking with me daily, not in Him making me have comfort and success. My life is now a living sacrifice paid for in blood.

1 Peter 4:12-13 (ESV) says it best:

> *"Beloved, do not be surprised at the fiery trial when it comes upon you to test you, as though something strange were happening to you. But rejoice insofar as you share Christ's sufferings, that you may also rejoice and be glad when his glory is revealed."*

Even in this suffering, there's growth and happiness. It's the cry of our hearts in the dark hours. It's the strength we have and the joy before us that we can holler about Him while suffering. I don't understand it all at times and certainly wouldn't complain if the Lord removed my cancer quickly. No one likes to suffer or watch someone they love suffer, but if we must, let Him be glorified.

As we rest in His sovereignty, we also reach for His promises. We know God is our healer. We know He still heals today, and we make our requests known to God according to Scripture:

> *"Do not be anxious about anything, but in everything by prayer and supplication with thanksgiving let your requests be made known to God."* **(Philippians 4:6 ESV)**

We plead with the Lord just as Jesus did:

> *"And going a little farther he fell on his face and prayed, saying, 'My Father, if it be possible, let this cup pass from me; nevertheless, not as I will, but as you will.'"* **(Matthew 26:39 ESV)**

I don't pretend to understand it all nor do I wish to minimize my situation or sugarcoat my struggle. There is a very real battle being waged in my life right now. But I know God is God, and I trust Him. I know He is faithful, and His will is being performed. I've always wanted my life to bring Him glory and for reasons only He knows.

It's like when the disciples asked Jesus why a man was blind in **John 9:1-3 (ESV)**:

> *"As He passed by, He saw a man blind from birth. And His disciples asked Him, 'Rabbi, who sinned, this man or his parents, that he was born blind?' Jesus answered, 'It was not that this man sinned, or his parents, but that the works of God might be displayed in him.'"*

The hope of my story is that the works of God will be displayed in me. Certainly, God will be glorified in a miracle healing and me walking away without so much suffering. However, if He requires me to walk through the valley and climb the mountain, He will be glorified as well. One way or another, I will be healed and whole.

The "how" question is one that's hard to explain. The "why" question will not even be entertained. Nausea, pain, and fatigue are relentless. Naturally, times of joy are hard to come by. Still, the goodness of God has sustained me.

He has showered me with love and support. The joy I experience can only come from the Lord. The peace He has given me truly passes all understanding. I am in a place of trust like I've never experienced, and I know God is with me—He proves it every day.

CHAPTER 10

NEW YORK CITY

I should have this figured out by now.

It's been eight months since I had cuss words thrown at me that knocked me off my feet. I'm one month out from having part of my left kidney removed due to the tumor growing faster than we liked. It was my fifth surgery since the diagnosis, and it seems things are getting worse.

Doctors keep telling me to stay patient and positive. "Keytruda takes time to work," they say.

But how much time? My body is ravaged, and my bank account is dry. I know I should remain positive and let my faith stand firm, but I'm growing tired.

This is a different tired than I've ever felt before. It's hard to explain this type of tiredness to someone that's never felt the effects of cancer treatments. I've worked hard my whole life. I played sports and was very active. I've been dragged around Disney World for seven straight days and felt tiredness that could cripple a marathon runner, but cancer fatigue is a new animal. And really, that's what doctors call it: "cancer fatigue."

Fatigue really isn't much different from tiredness, except how it attacks you. Tiredness creeps up on you and comes on gradually. Fatigue is like a wall that suddenly smacks you in the face. You could be feeling fine, full of energy, and perky, and then suddenly, you feel completely flat, like a possum on an old back road. It's definitely not helped by long days or stress.

I have to listen to my body a lot more and not be so keen to accept all those invitations to go out, speak at events, or hold book signing appearances. I love each of those things, but I pay for them soon after. It's about pacing yourself more and not feeling guilty if you need to change plans, but I've had trouble with that my entire life. I could have a weekend of birthday parties, yard work, church outings, and family gatherings, and if someone asked me to help them cut down trees, I'd say, "Sure, man! I have nothing going on. I'll be right over."

That's my DNA. My dad was the same way. He never rested because so many people relied on him to be their "fix it" person. He grew old quickly, but he was happy. He found his "normal" in helping people, and I believe that if he ever stopped, he'd think his purpose was missing.

I am much the same way. I enjoy helping people. I enjoy gatherings. I want to hug folks. I want to laugh. I want to tell dad jokes and eat casseroles until my feet swell. But at times, I can feel those things taking their toll on me.

Sometimes, it's simply a case of sitting down and giving in to it. Not in a negative way—just going with it and not fighting. The sooner you do that, the sooner (hopefully) you'll come through it and feel perky again.

That's difficult if I'm in a situation where I can't go to bed or sit on the sofa, like if I'm at work. I feel that wall of fatigue hit me, and I think, *What do I do?*

I've tried changing things in my life, but it hasn't been easy. Old habits are hard to break. I aim to get eight hours of sleep a night. Rarely do I get more than three. Writing is my escape from the tricks our minds play on us, so I've reduced stress by writing more. I also exercise because it's a great de-stressor, and . . .

Okay. You got me. I haven't exercised since the invention of TV dinners.

Still, the "new me" is so much more self-aware.

I used to slow down two days after I should have. Now, I feel the fatigue coming and I think to myself, *Get to bed early, make time, cancel out the evening. You can always arrange it for next week. Have an early dinner and an early night and focus on sleep.*

I think, for me, the hardest part of fatigue is the mental side. Months before the diagnosis, I felt tired for no reason. I realize now that I was utterly exhausted and already ill.

It's not good when fatigue hits, but I'm not going to panic about it. Instead, I think, *What am I going to do about it?*

I know I can't just keep pushing like I've always done, so I usually rest, read, and write. That's really helped me cope with the uncertainty of fatigue because I don't know how long it's going to last. It might be an hour, it might last until I go to bed, or it could be for days on end.

So, I say to myself, "It's okay. What can I do? Can I rest? Am I somewhere where I can close my eyes for half an hour?" and I don't get in a flap. The more I get in a flap about it, the worse it gets, particularly if I'm tired because that makes it seem a hundred times worse.

I feel like I need to make an allowance for fatigue in my life, so I do. Firstly, it's about physically trying to avoid fatigue coming on. Secondly, it's about mentally accepting that fatigue is something I have to come to terms with. It's part of my new life, one that has drastically changed me.

I begin researching cancer fatigue like I'm doing a term paper, except there are fewer ramen noodles and no dorm rooms. I find several articles, but nobody talks about a cure. There are vitamin suggestions, dietary plans, and even some millennial antidotes made from coconut milk and roasted beetles found in the Amazon. I've steered clear of insect remedies so far but short of home remedies, I'm willing to try anything at this point.

See, I learned my lesson regarding home remedies at an early age. My uncle was stressing about an upcoming doctor's appointment he had to go to in order to keep his job. He knew his cholesterol was out of whack and his kidneys weren't acting right. He couldn't lose his job over stuff like that. More importantly, he feared the doctor would take him off of cheeseburgers and Wild Turkey.

Mom suggested something to get his cholesterol in check before the big day. "Oatmeal will lower your cholesterol. My doctor told me that."

My uncle, being the intelligent guy he was, took her advice. For the next two weeks leading up to his appointment, he ate nothing but oatmeal . . . for every meal. He wasn't taking any chances. The thought of no quarter-pounders and bourbon was just downright scary.

Now, I said he was intelligent, but he was also as southern as a bluetick hound dog. To make his oatmeal enjoyable, he covered it in butter, brown sugar, and Golden Eagle Syrup. Two weeks later, he was put on sugar pills and told he needed to lose twenty pounds.

You can find anything on the Internet. Even treatments for lymphatic cancers. The treatments are not yet approved, but they could be your lifesaver. And that's just what I think I've found.

IN MY ADVENTURES roaming the world wide web, I keep getting drawn to one particular clinical trial that seems to perfectly fit me. I discuss it with my doctors. They're aware of the trial.

"It's a long shot," they tell me. "Only a couple hundred will be selected out of thousands of applicants."

My luck hasn't been the greatest lately, so I'm reluctant to say anything to anyone because, well, I'm not sure if this thing will even happen. But I go along with all the medical releases, phone interviews, and lab work. And I wait. When the news I've been waiting for comes, I'm floored. I've been accepted!

I'm still in the "pinch me, is this real" stage. But now, after speaking with an amazing team of doctors, I realize this trial may be my miracle—it is specifically designed for treating cancer cells in the lymphoid system, which is where my trouble lies.

Doctors will harvest good stuff from one of my tumors, give it steroids and make it work out, and then they'll put it back in me to kick the bad stuff's butt. It's kinda like a WWE training ground but without terrible acting and commercials.

That's in layman's terms so folks like me can understand it. For all you folks with doctorate degrees and a bunch of letters after your name, here's what the doctors say:

"Lifileucel is called 'autologous tumor-infiltrating lymphocytes' (TIL) therapy. TIL therapies are made in a laboratory from white blood cells called lymphocytes (or T cells) that will be collected from the patient's tumor. Lifileucel is designed to selectively attack cancer cells while leaving healthy cells alone."

This cancer-butt-kicking party will take place at the Memorial Sloan Kettering Cancer Center in Manhattan. *New York!* That alone is scary!

I've heard stories about cab drivers that moonlight as serial killers. I've been told the folks are rude and it's against the law to smile. And get this: no sweet tea. None! How do they survive? Better yet, how will I survive?

Treatments will be monthly. Travel and lodging are all on my dime, which is *a lot*. It will be like spending the equivalent of taking a vacation . . . but every month. I also learn that I'll meet my team of lifesavers in New York the week of December 12th through the 15th.

So, why change things this far into treatment? What makes this trial so much better? How will I afford it?

There are many questions I ask myself. Truthfully, I prayed God would show me a path to being healthy again. Perhaps this is it. If I could have got in earlier, I would have but it is all in His timing. I'm just glad I got the call at all.

Immunotherapy treatments will continue back in Alabama. The new treatment will be an added bonus. It's kinda like strawberry shortcake. It's already good, but when you add whip cream, it takes it up a notch.

The immunotherapy treatment I've been doing since April isn't getting the full results I'd hoped for. Two new tumors have formed. This new treatment in New York gives me added hope that we can kick cancer's hindquarters and be done with it.

This is it, I tell myself. *This will be my saving grace.*

THE NEWS BREAKS QUICKLY.

My wife has to get a new coat. "I only have Alabama winter coats. Everyone knows you must have a new coat when you go to New York."

I'm still trying to find out how we're going to get there. My daughter Emilee is mapping out shoe stores and perfume shops. Dawson, my son, took a trip a few months prior for the Macy's Thanksgiving Day parade, so he opts out of this extravaganza.

Airline tickets are expensive. For what it would cost all three of us to fly, we could buy a two-bedroom cabin with central heating and air and still have enough left over for the complete Lynyrd Skynyrd box set.

I call Delta and tell them my circumstances, hoping for a discount. The price goes up. I explain that I don't want to fly the plane, maybe just sit in the aisle. I don't even need a seat, complimentary peanuts, or a parachute. To cover the expenses, it's suggested I sell something. Like a kidney . . . which I only have one good one.

After a lot of prayer, thought, and searching Google with questions such as "How much can I sell half a kidney for?", we elect to drive. We're aware that New York City is eight light-years away, but it's still much cheaper than flying. Besides, everything my daughter already wants to bring back would cost as much as another ticket if it flew with us.

We research things to do in New York. It's Christmastime, and we know it will be beautiful. The Rockefeller Center Christmas tree is definitely on the list, as are Chinatown, Little Italy, the 9/11 Memorial and Museum, and the Statue of Liberty. We also want to see Central Park. It's amazing to me that such a large getaway into nature exists between buildings so tall the moon routinely bumps into them when passing by.

Two weeks zoom by in a flash with us making our preparations. I even downloaded a cuss word translator; I was practicing so that I could fit in, but the app wasn't as advertised. The translator didn't understand hillbilly and ended up walking out on me on the second day of practice.

Then the day finally arrives. We've packed, boarded our pup, and gassed up the four-wheel cross-country-mobile for an adventure that awaits us in a land of snow and ticked-off cab drivers. We're leaving the valley of sweet tea and warm weather for the asphalt of double-cuss words and sub-freezing temps.

I've packed a toboggan, gloves, insulated socks, and a wood-burning heater. Kristy and Emilee have travel pillows. I also have a triple-shot convenience store can of coffee and a bag of beef jerky, so I should be good for an entire tank of gas.

It's early. We're leaving town before sunrise. We've got a long way to go, so any time made in the dark is double-bonus points.

The interstate looks different at four in the morning. There are eighteen-wheelers keeping America going and dads trying to beat the GPS time. Nobody is racing to get to work, little league games, or meat sales at the Piggly Wiggly. Everybody is just cruising while listening to their passengers snore. Here, I am in my element.

The GPS tells me I will arrive in fifteen hours and twenty-seven minutes if I don't stop for gas, bathrooms, or tacos. I take that as a challenge. I can name that tune in under fifteen flat, no sweat. I take to the open highway like a souped-up possum.

Alabama roadways are beautiful. There are forests, rivers, and potholes that have historic markers stuck in them. This underprivileged American highway has been my home for half a century. I've traveled interstates, back roads, and dirt roads from one end to the other, top to bottom. I've carried on conversations with highway state troopers and shared fish bait with total strangers who ate tomatoes straight from the plant.

I love this state. Namely, because it will always be my home. Alabama is where I cut my teeth and learned to drive on roads that took me to faraway countries, like Atlanta. You don't recognize its true beauty until you drive it early in the morning and watch the sun come up, the fog lift, and deer bounce off Pontiacs.

It's not the glamourous Route 66, winding through the untamed west like a stray purebred. Neither is it Highway 98 that runs across the Florida panhandle, teasing you with the coastline and the smell of fresh seafood.

The Alabama roads that I travel are more like the cousin you see at family reunions, the one who always stands in the corner, silently drinking his Budweiser Heavy. Most folks forget he's even there—which is too bad; if you were to actually talk to this cousin, you'd realize that not only is he pretty interesting and polite, but he can also make you thankful for other cousins out there who are different.

These cousin roads travel through charming little towns like Fort Payne, Mentone, and Muscle Shoals, where the greats like Aretha Franklin and Mick Jagger hollered in studios.

Some people say it's best to stay on the interstate and not use the back roads. "Just fly through Alabama unless you need to stop for beef jerky," they say. They're also missing a lot of what God created when He was in a good mood.

Our path takes us through the corner of Georgia. We cut the edge off like it's the bite of icing on a cake we want to sample.

You're in cousin territory in north Georgia. You start noticing mountains here. You're up and down hills so much that your transmission smokes. We travel between Lookout Mountain and Sand Mountain, a place so pretty it will make your teeth hurt.

We catch traffic just past Chattanooga. An Amazon truck lost a fight with a Honda right around the Hiwassee River. Traffic is tangled up like barbed wire being drug through a hayfield. I'm losing the minutes I gained on my GPS, and it causes anxiety so bad I have to find a station that plays the soothing sounds of Willie Nelson.

Once around the delivery issue, we cruise right on through the home state of Dolly Parton, Davy Crockett, and Morgan Freeman in no time. After a bathroom break and a restock on Skittles, our Jeep Cherokee makes its first appearance in our country's tenth state, Virginia.

In Virginia, the highway seems to straighten out. We make time by singing the wrong lyrics to country songs and drafting behind long-haul truck drivers. Before we know it, we look up and the sign tells us we are entering West Virginia. Blue Ridge Mountains, Shenandoah River, and the untamed Potomac . . .

As soon as we pass the state line, every radio station is required to play "Take Me Home, Country Roads" by John Denver at least once an hour—twice during rush hour. We haven't seen a NASCAR bumper sticker since Tennessee, but here they hand them out each year with car tag renewals.

Maryland comes into view. We only catch a piece of it, but

Maryland is known for some of my favorite things. Take, for instance, its crabs from Chesapeake Bay; blue crabs in particular. The state is also known for being the birthplace of the National Anthem. In 1802, an invention called the refrigerator came from here. Soon after, canned beer arrived. Grass couldn't get cut after that. Divorce rates skyrocketed. Casseroles were saved for weeks at a time and almost put Chef Boyardee out of business.

Up to bat next is Pennsylvania. I used to think Philadelphia was the entire state. I was wrong. It is much more. This is a state with a whole bunch of Amish jellies and wood chairs for sale at every Texaco station. There's Amish butter, Amish salsa, and Amish TV dinners you heat on pot-belly stoves. There are handmade slingshots, pop guns, and even wood-carved Plymouths being pulled by quarter horses.

Pennsylvania is beautiful. This is settlers' land. Some of our first fine folks from across the pond decided to show up here and never go back. Why would they?

The mountainsides are blanketed in flowing grass that moves like the ocean. Each grain field is dotted with trees that have survived hundreds of years and the threat of a Buc-ees showing up and claiming its right to the land. Each two-story, three-family home and every wood barn, ancient schoolhouse, dilapidated pickup, and grain silo looks to be from a painting you'd find at a five-star flea market. It's picturesque.

I can hardly focus on the electric cars and diesel log trucks surrounding me. It's easy to forget your troubles when you're driving through 200 years of history that's immune to Starbucks and CNN.

"Have you ever seen anything so beautiful?" my wife asks.

No. I have not.

Unless you count Alabama in the seventies, when our family reunions were so large we were considered for incorporation into a municipality; back when cousins outnumbered bill collectors and uncles told the best stories from wrap-around porches. We played football between kudzu patches and drank from garden hoses. That was beautiful, and it always will be.

The beauty we're driving through is a different type of beauty. There are rolling hills and flowing meadows. These horse-drawn

carriages and pickups have been raised to work. I want to stop and take pictures every ten miles . . . but that GPS time is taunting me.

This is my first visit to Pennsylvania, and nobody prepared me for what it would look like. In fact, I feel downright silly trying to describe to you all that I'm seeing. This looks like the middle of nowhere but *better*. This blacktop slices through a portion of America that I've only seen on postcards and cable television.

The further into the state we drive, the more I like it. There are 8,000 miles of fence. And old homes! I've never seen so many ancient American farmhouses. Many of these homesteads sit on hills overlooking Beulah Land.

We've driven right at 1,000 miles at this point. Allentown, Pennsylvania seems like a nice place to pitch a tent for the night. We're just a few hours away from New York City and could make it in one day but choose not to—mainly because our reservations aren't until the next day but also because I want one more night to freshen up on my Big Apple-approved cuss words.

OUR HOTEL IS NOTHING FANCY. It's your basic interstate deal, but it's clean. There's even a continental breakfast that will get us on our way in the morning. We check in and ask about a good local place to grab dinner. The young clerk recommends Starbucks.

"Oh, I almost forgot that the next exit has a new McDonald's!" she exclaims excitedly. "It has phone chargers built into the tables."

It's hard to pass up built-in phone chargers, but we decide to forage for ourselves in the surrounding uncharted wilderness. We find a P. F. Chang's and decide we'll dive into the flavor of the wild Asian cuisine of Northern Pennsylvania. The noodles are great, the pepper steak is charcoal, and the spicy chicken is hot enough to put down a warthog. But they have sweet tea, so we compromise and tip accordingly.

The next morning, I wake before Kristy and Emilee and slip out of the room to go sniff out coffee and read about how the world is doing.

The lobby is already crowded. I hear chatter as soon as the elevator doors open. I knew there would be a few folks up and going, but it seems like more than usual. After all, this is the moment of day when guests emerge from rooms with messed-up hair, house shoes, and pajama pants, much like a trip to the Walmart.

Folks shuffle through corridors toward coffee machines like the living dead. I smell the aroma of coffee mixed with artificial scrambled eggs and meat-like sausage links.

"Look, Mom!" a small child shouts. "It's a blizzard!"

I walk around the corner so that I can see through the lobby windows. It's snowing! Not like Alabama snow. This is coming down so hard you can't see across the parking lot. While I slept and fought spicy chicken heartburn, the Pennsylvania sky dumped a blanket on us that would shut down the South for two football seasons.

I call Kristy back in our room.

No answer.

I call again.

No answer.

I've started back to the elevator when my phone rings.

"Look outside!" I answer, hollering like a seven-year-old. "It's snowing! Like a lot! We can build a snowman and eat milk sandwiches it's snowing so hard!"

"What?" she replies in her still-half-asleep voice.

"Just *look!*" I yell through my smartphone.

This is the type of snow we've heard about but have never experienced. We usually spend three days hoarding groceries and firewood for the dusting we get overnight that's gone by early morning. Not this! Everything here is covered, and it's still coming down.

"What do we do?" Kristy asks. "We can't drive in this."

The interstate is close enough that I can see traffic still moving. All I have to do is get up the on-ramp and follow the professionals.

I can do this, I tell myself with the confidence of a button on a fat guy's sports coat.

❦

AFTER MANDATORY PICTURES of us in the snow, a cup of lukewarm coffee, six meat-like sausage links, and a few prayers, we are on our way.

The interstate is tricky. If you stay on the tracks, driving is easy. Changing lanes, however, is like a baby giraffe standing for the first time.

Three hours of praying later . . .

Welcome to New York! But just the state. We aren't in the city yet.

I always thought that as soon as you crossed the state line, you had your picture made with the Statue of Liberty. I've never seen this part of New York on calendars. It's much like Pennsylvania. In fact, if Pennsylvania finished college and moved out of New York's home and into the trailer behind it, this would be it. It's still the same-looking yard.

The interstate weaves you through picturesque images that many folks don't associate with the Empire State. This is the unsung part of this country. Nobody mentions New York farmland.

Cows! They have *cows* here. Why didn't anybody tell me New York had cows? I bet they "moo" in a Yankee accent.

But this scene doesn't last. Before long, the trees give way to concrete and steel. Cows turn into taxicabs, and from seemingly nowhere, hotdog stands run by retired cab drivers appear.

Welcome to New York City! The city that never sleeps . . . because there are too many horns honking.

At least it's friendly here. I'm driving through streets about as wide as a baby grand piano while people honk at me and wave. We take pictures of everything as we drive into the city. Kristy takes pictures of pizza places, designer purse stores, skyscrapers, police on horses, and other drivers telling us we're Number One.

Next, we drive through the Holland Tunnel. We are *under* a river! A whole dadgum river! The Hudson River separates us from the world above. How in the world is this possible? Did they build the tunnel and then God added water? It goes so far under that our radio gives up the spirit and Tom Petty quits hollering.

When we emerge back into the sunlight, it looks like every building has been fertilized with extra-strength MiracleGro and has shot straight through the clouds. More pictures are taken. More horns sing. Plenty of one-finger salutes are added to the parade.

We hang out of the windows like Labradors on a Sunday drive. Streets get even more narrow. We fold in our mirrors and smile. Nobody smiles back.

We're staying at a hotel at Grand Central Station, which is one of the busiest places in New York. Over 750,000 folks go through this place every day. It's like stepping into a fire ant bed.

Nobody stops. Nobody speaks unless they're yelling at you for taking pictures and you're in their way, or they're ordering a hotdog. For someone who grew up in a town of less than a thousand, it is a crazy sight to see.

There's also nowhere to park, so we pull up streetside in front of our hotel. A concierge runs to the car and asks if we're checking in.

"Yes," I tell him.

He whistles and a team of bag handlers appear from all directions. They're grabbing our bags, helping us from the car, and before I can even grab my half-eaten bag of pretzels, our car zips away and we're standing here wondering how we became homeless in under three seconds.

When we finally catch up to our bags, a bellhop hands us a paper ticket. "This is to get your car back from the valet."

"How much is that?" I ask.

"Not much. Only eighty dollars a night, plus a service fee. Oh, and a New York State parking tax."

"Well, is that gonna cost me a bunch?"

"Maybe not," he says.

"Maybe?"

"Maybe *not . . .?*" he stresses.

He stands in front of me, holding out his hand. I shake it firmly. He looks at me in a funny accent.

"He wants a tip, honey," my wife explains.

"For what? Telling me I have to buy my car back when we're ready to go home?" I ask them.

I pull out my wallet and hand him a five. He peers at it and clears his throat. I shake my head and stare back into my wallet. The smallest I have is a twenty. I hand it to him.

"Thank you, sir," he says as he turns to walk away. He pauses and adds, "Oh, and there's another fee we use from the parking deck that'll be added on."

I've only been in New York for ten minutes, yet I've already paid someone to carjack me and now I find out it will cost me what seems like $600 a day to buy my car back. I miss Alabama.

❦

OUR HOTEL IS NICE, and our room is one toward the top. We can see passenger jets flying two floors below our window. The highest I've ever been up in a building was when I was a kid and we snuck through the gates to climb the fire watch tower on the north end of my hometown. From that tower, we could see three trailer parks and two bootleggers. From where we're staying in this hotel, we can see Chicago.

We quickly claim beds just before our luggage arrives in our room. The bag boy is a polite young man. He recognizes our Southern accent and asks where we were from.

"Alabama," we proudly tell him.

"Do you guys really hunt your own food?" he asks.

"We do," I reply. "But for us, we usually find it at the Piggly Wiggly."

"The Piggly Wiggly?"

"It's a grocery store," Kristy explains.

He takes our last bag off the cart and places it in our room. He then stands, hands clasped together, at our door, and stares at me.

"Thanks, man!" I holler.

"Honey, a tip," Kristy says as she raises her brow at me.

So far, I haven't even stepped foot in a restaurant, store, clinic, cab, or subway and I'm out fifty bucks in just *tips*. It's only been fifteen minutes and I am going broke!

No wonder it costs so much to live here. Everybody gets tips for everything. I'm afraid to buy a drink from the vending machine at this point. I'm sure the price will be five bucks for the drink and a twenty-dollar tip to the guy who stocks the machine.

OUR DAY GOES WELL, and we see a lot of sights.

The Macy's Department Store is huge. Nine floors of bedding, toys, accessories, and designer under britches. Santa was there but we had to have a reservation to see him. The North Pole has gone high-tech, and if you didn't get an email from Leonardo the Head Elf, you aren't getting past Bruno, the world's tallest toy maker.

New York City is even bigger than I imagined. I snap pictures faster than the paparazzi at a Britney Spears court hearing. I haven't been this amazed since they added disco lights to Bryant-Denny Stadium.

We go to Chanel, where I'm followed by a security guard that looks like he belongs in the Secret Service. I don't know if it's due to my hillbilly accent or because I asked where the channel locks were located as we were being escorted into the store.

I see shirts with prices higher than some Oldsmobiles. There are shoes on shelves that cost more than a bass boat. My daughter wants a bottle of perfume.

"Sure," I agree.

I don't think it should cost more than fifty or sixty bucks, but I about go into a full seizure when my credit card is swiped.

Next, we walk by Tiffany and Company. I tremble at the thought of my wife and daughter getting loose in there. Saks Fifth Avenue is on the list. Louis Vuitton, Gucci, Rolex, Dolce & Gabbana, Prada, Armani, Fendi, Versace, Cartier: they're all right here on Fifth Avenue, and I am a nervous wreck.

It's getting dark now, so we start our walk back to our tip-collecting hotel, which is only a few blocks away, but New York blocks seem like different zip codes.

We stop by the Rockefeller Center and stand in amazement at the gigantic Christmas tree. It is beautiful. If Heaven puts up a tree every year, I hope it looks like this one. I'm told it's a Norway spruce. It is eighty-four feet tall and has over 50,000 LED lights. I'm like a kid again looking at it.

The next day: more sightseeing. Chinatown is on the list. A guy chases me down and offers me a genuine Rolex watch for a hundred bucks.

"This real-deal," he says.

"Are you sure?" I ask. "Rolex should only have one 'x' in it, shouldn't it?"

"Limited edition," he insists. "Worth way more than one you buy in store."

"Then why are you selling it so cheap?" I inquire as I look it over. "This thing sells for like $25,000 on Fifth Avenue."

"I had coupon. Today your lucky day."

I decide to pass. He chases. Others join in.

We're being chased by ladies with twenty-dollar Louis Vuitton purses, five-dollar Ray-Ban sunglasses, and one dude even has knock-off Zebco 33 fishing reels. I could get into buying thirty-dollar Air Jordan sneakers, but I draw the line when you try to sell me a fake Zebco.

We visit Little Italy, where we eat some of the best lobster ravioli to ever be set before me. I try to buy some of their signature sauce but am unsuccessful. I produce some southern charm, and the owner ends up giving me a free quart of their secret family recipe sauce, which he claims he's never done for anyone before.

It just goes to show you what kindness and a smile can do. It's powerful, and when you add a dash of Alabama accent, we dang near can conquer the world, or at least lower Manhattan.

We visit a few landmarks and shop at a sneaker store, where Emilee loads up on hard-to-find high-tops. We take more pictures and ride with Uber drivers with foreign accents. Then we make our way back to a fine dining establishment across from our hotel that goes by the name of McDonald's, where we all get our side dishes super-sized.

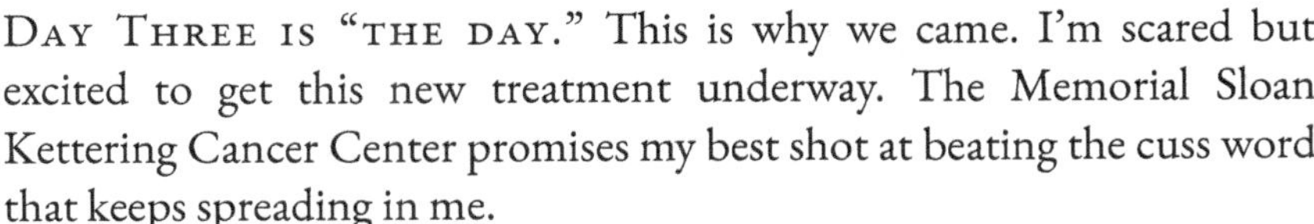

DAY THREE IS "THE DAY." This is why we came. I'm scared but excited to get this new treatment underway. The Memorial Sloan Kettering Cancer Center promises my best shot at beating the cuss word that keeps spreading in me.

I wake up at 4:00 AM. I have to be there by 6:00. It's only a mile and a half away, but I want to arrive early.

It's cold. Snow flurries accumulate in my hair. Horns honk at me, but I don't know why. I'm on the sidewalk. A man is trying to sell me a hotdog at 4:30 in the morning. I'm so confused. I'm not used to anything I just mentioned.

I decide my best chance of making it there without frostbite and hotdog heartburn is to take a taxi. I grab the first one that drives by. He lets me know he'll give me a better deal if I pay with cash. No problem. The Uber was going to charge me twenty-five bucks to go a mile and a half. So, he takes me and drops me off for only forty bucks. I hate New York math.

The first place I go to at this medical institute is not the correct location. I'm sent somewhere else. That's okay. I'm early because I'm used to being wrong. I prepare for failure. It's something I've learned to prepare for because it finds me often.

I do have a confession, though: I was wrong about New York.

I was told horror stories about New Yorkers. Folks said they would holler at you for no reason. I heard cab drivers were straight from Hades, or worse. I was warned street vendors would try to rip you off and sell you bona fide Italian designer purses made in an apartment in Queens. I was told they would cuss you for being too slow, too tall, too Baptist. I believed all these stories and even the ones I saw on television.

They're just not true. Not everyone is like that.

Sure, Chinatown had me convinced for a while, but since then, I haven't been cursed in any languages. Maybe those people are still sleeping. Perhaps I haven't met them yet. It's only Day Three. But I've been told "good morning" so many times already that I have no choice but to believe it will be.

The ladies checking in people here at the cancer center treat me like royalty. I'm offered bottled water, coffee, and Netflix logins. I almost think they have me confused for someone important. I've never been important in my life.

There's a kid in the waiting room, and I can't help but notice the little guy. He's frail but full of life. His eyes have circles around them darker than a coal miner's, but he can't sit still. He asks his mom questions in rapid-fire:

"Will it hurt?"

"No, baby," she lies.

"Will they poke me again, Momma?"

"Maybe not, sweetie." —*Liar.*

"Do I have to lay in that tube again?"

"It's possible, baby. But this time will be quicker." —*Habitual storyteller!*

"Momma?"

"Yes, baby?"

"Am I gonna die?"

Silence.

I've listened to these complete strangers' entire conversation. Here and now, I feel like this little boy is my kid. That last question stops me like a Chinatown shoe vendor. A lump sits in my throat. My eyes are leaking. It must be the bottled water.

At this point, I want him to be cured more than I want myself to be cured. I hate having cancer, but this kid … any kid … This ain't fair.

I walk over and tell his mother that I'd like to give him a wristband and ask if it's okay. She smiles and tells me it is.

His name is Brandon. He's proud of the scar that runs down the back of his neck. He makes sure I see it. He pulls the neckline of his shirt down.

"See! It goes all the way to here," he exclaims.

"Brandon," his mom yells. "Leave him alone. I'm sure he has enough to worry about."

No. In fact, I don't. I want to hear more about this kid.

I ask Brandon about his favorite thing to do in New York. He says his favorite thing is Lego World. He tells me about the Lego dragon that's bigger than him.

Bigger. That's a word I like to focus on.

Within a few minutes, Brandon has nine of the "God Is Bigger" bracelets I brought with me. After I gave him and his mom theirs, he told me he has eight friends on his seven-year-old church basketball team. They're playing for the league championship next weekend. Brandon thinks the little bands will help them win. I do, too.

Brandon tells me he won't play in the big game. He can't any longer. His bones are fragile from cancer. He's sick from the treatments. Brandon wants to play, but his mom said he can't. He plans on being there, though.

"We are a team," he tells me with a huge smile.

Cancer doesn't play fair.

It makes you feel like a flat possum 90 percent of the time. It cancels parties. It drains bank accounts. You lose friends because they don't know how to act around you. It forces you to wait in cold hospital rooms until your name is called. You listen to little kids tell you how they used to play basketball but would now give anything just to be out there with their teammates.

Cancer is horrible.

———••◦∞◦••———

MY NAME IS CALLED. It's my turn. I've been here less than twenty minutes and they have me ready for inspection. This place is more efficient than a Chick-fil-A.

I'm in a gown that highlights my knobby knees and hindquarters. The technicians and nurses take turns asking me to say things like "y'all" and "aight" and "sweet tea."

"Guess where he's from," a nurse hollers to another before turning to me and adding, "Say it again and see if she can guess it right."

"Y'all sure are nice," I say through laughter.

"Tennessee!" contestant number two shouts.

"Nope," her friend says.

"Kentucky?"

"Not it!"

"Virginia," she continues. "No, West Virginia."

"Alabama! He's a *real* Alabama boy," nurse number one hollers. She just couldn't stand it any longer.

They get more folks. Before long, I'm bare-butted in a room full of accent-aholic strangers. I know how the monkeys at the zoo feel. A custodian even joins the party. He asks if we really eat barbecue and collards all the time.

I assure him, "Absolutely not, only on special occasions."

Then my doctor enters. Everyone's faces get serious. Nurses no longer play guessing games, but my hindquarters are still cold sitting on the exam table.

The doctor tells me what we'll be doing. She says things like "long-term side effects" and "harvesting." She throws big words at me. I nod like I actually understand them. She says she thinks this trial will work. She's almost certain.

Almost.

Thinks.

This has been a long few months of "almosts" and "I thinks" littered with a few "maybes" and "lets hopes." I've also heard doctors say things like, "I really thought this would work."

At this point, I've had five surgeries in eight months. I've lost weight because I literally have fewer body parts. But I have my own words that I'm using. They aren't the "almosts" or terms even belonging to that linguistic family. My words are "God is bigger," and I make sure words like "faith" and "prayer" and "smile" are part of my daily vocabulary.

But . . .

There were a few days when I used words that really got to me. Those words were "what if."

Immunotherapy was supposed to take care of things. So far, it has not. There's yet another tumor that just joined the party. Treatments were working for a while. You know . . . *almost.*

"I ask all my patients this," the doc tells me. "What do you expect from this clinical trial?"

I'm caught off guard. I spent all my time learning the correct names of my prescriptions. I wasn't prepared for a question like this.

I don't know, I have no idea what I expect. I barely understand what it is that I have. I'm just learning how to flag down a taxi and not get in a fight over who gets it. I guess I should have been focusing on other things.

I reckon I expect to live long enough to see grandkids. I hope, one day, I don't feel this way. I want to have plenty of energy again. I want to be able to enjoy things and not physically pay for it at the end of the day.

This cuss word has changed me, and I hate most of those changes. It also created some changes that I've embraced. I cherish every waking minute now. Time is so valuable. My family time means even more. If I knew I would grow this close to God, I would have carried this burden many years before now.

I wish I were a good enough writer to explain what cancer has done for my spiritual walk and closeness to Christ, but I'm not. You're just going to have to trust me on this one when I tell you that I've never had so much peace in my life.

That's only the start of what I could say when the doctor asks what I expect. That's what I wish I'd started with.

I don't. All that comes out is, "I hope it works."

Hope. That's like one level up from "almost."

But she's asked what I expect.

I guess what I expect is already happening. I expect God to do something big. After all, remember that New Year's Eve prayer: *"Do something big in my life that glorifies You!"*

See, it doesn't even have to be to me that something big happens to. For all I care, He can simply use me for the big things that need to happen. I've already told dozens of people in New York about my Savior. I've given out over 100 "God Is Bigger" wristbands in Times Square, and I'm just getting started. I want everyone in New York to have one. I'm trying. Lord's willing and the creek don't rise, I'll succeed.

But what do I want?

Man, I could go on for days about this.

I want to beat this. I don't want to have to take treatments any longer.

More than that, I want folks to know that no matter what we're faced with, we can use it for God's glory. I want to grow even closer to Him. To encourage others. I want God to be glorified through this battle. If I must endure it, something big will come from it. I just know it will!

I'm taking it a day at a time. That's all I can do.

New York has something that's offered me a chance. I have hope this is going to work. I have faith that it will. And by "work," I mean that whatever God intends to use this for will happen. Whatever the outcome, I win.

WHEN I THINK MORE about it, I want folks to believe that New Yorkers are nothing like what the news tells you. They are good people. I bet the right ones would even eat cornbread with you.

I want to come back when I'm not enrolled as a guinea pig. I want to eat New York pizza, the good kind like Joe's which claims to be the best. I ate pizza inside Macy's on our first day here. That wasn't the New York pizza in the commercials.

I want to walk the city, see the sights, and buy fake sunglasses from a duffle bag. I want to meet more New Yorkers. The ones I've met so far are nice, so let's make this a trend. I want to do them a favor, like make southern sweet tea for them. I want to do *all* that.

I want kids like Brandon to be able to play basketball. I want them to win their championship games. When they do, I want them to hold up their hands so everybody can see their wristbands. Then they will all know what Brandon already knows.

They'll know the reason why this living hell Brandon and I are going through is so worth it. It's three little words: God is bigger!

And no matter what, we *will* win!

CHAPTER 11

LOOK AT GOD!

"**M**an, how can you stay so positive dealing with all this mess?" A friend is quizzing me on the use of illegal drugs. "You're always smiling and shouting about how good God is, but you have cancer. Are you on some good stuff?"

My answer is simple. I've been on, and am still on, some *very* good stuff. It's called "faith."

I've seen the transformation of those that have gone through life-altering illnesses. I have witnessed both sides of it—the good and the bad. Although I've been chasing Christ for many years, it's brought me to a new level of trusting Him.

Things changed, for me, in literally one day. One minute, we were talking and laughing, and the next, there was silence. We were in disbelief. I had a lot of "how" and "why" questions, but more than anything, I found solace in the quietness. I wouldn't even have to go to God for the answers; it seemed like He was ahead of me and putting verses and devotionals in place to prepare me for what lay ahead.

In the silence, I knew I had to trust God with whatever was happening and going to happen. I knew that if my time on this earth was cut short, I was ready for eternity with Jesus. Instead of panic, there was silence. Oddly, there was a lot of peace.

The morning following my diagnosis, my devotional Scripture was:

"And the peace of God, which surpasses all understanding, will guard your hearts and minds in Christ Jesus." **(Philippians 4:7 ESV)**

How could that not be God working on my behalf to tell the devil to take refuge elsewhere?

I'd memorized that verse early in my journey with Christ. However, I never could capture what it meant until that day. That moment with everything completely out of my control was beyond my understanding, but the peace that invaded my soul guarded my heart and my mind.

I know Jesus is with me and for me, regardless of the circumstances or the outcome, and I know that if God has a miracle in my future, He's already working on it. And if, by chance, I'm to be called home, I'm ready.

Some people struggle to believe in miracles. I've never really had that issue, but for much of my life, I thought miracles were for someone else. However, on the day I got my diagnosis, I felt my miracle would come . . . but when?

I've witnessed miracles my whole life. I saw cars totally ripped apart in accidents, yet the occupants walked away unscathed. Some would say it was only good engineering that saved them. I say otherwise.

At age seven, I learned what a miracle *really* was. I also learned how you qualify for one.

It was a Sunday night in 1979, and I was outside at the TV antenna with a pipe wrench. In other words, I was Dad's remote.

Back in that day and age, good television reception meant turning the fifty-foot antenna to face the station broadcasting a hundred miles away. Satellite dishes were already a thing, but they were the size of an Olympic swimming pool and cost as much as a Cadillac. We couldn't afford one. Even if we could, the housing projects probably wouldn't let us strap it to the apartment we called home.

"Right there! Leave it!" Dad hollered from inside.

I came back in and reclaimed my place on the floor with twenty of my best Hot Wheels. It was drive-in night for my collection of one-day dreams.

It hadn't been a bad channel change. In fact, it went smoothly. I'd undergone channel change missions in the middle of thunderstorms that took out half the south's power grids, but that one was a piece of cake. I felt accomplished. It's something I still list on my resume.

Dad had our TV tuned to a Donny and Marie Osmond special. He'd waited for it to come on since reading about it in the fall special of the *TV Guide*. He even circled it and pregamed from the cooler that sat beside his TV-watching chair.

Dad was about eight Budweisers into a six-pack when they performed his favorite, "Angel Love." He knew every word. While he hollered like Conway Twitty on a sold-out stage, I waited patiently for my turn.

Sundays were always the night I got my bath early and waited for the magic to come through the twenty-seven-inch console that weighed as much as Dad's Chevy Nova. "The Wonderful World of Disney" would come on next! That night was one of my favorites— "The Apple Dumpling Gang."

Don Knotts and Tim Conway were soon doing their best to make me laugh so uncontrollably that I almost wrecked a Hot Wheel. That's when it happened. Seven-year-old me heard a wheezing sound from Dad.

I thought Don Knotts made him blow a laughing gasket, so I laughed, too—more at the sound Dad was making—and I turned to acknowledge that we were both laughing. Father and son laughing together! That great invention took place somewhere around the birth of the automobile, but my laugh quickly turned to fear. Dad was the color of red you only see inside over-ripe watermelons. He was slumped in the chair, holding his chest.

Fifteen minutes later, paramedics were loading him into an ambulance, and I was standing on the porch, clutching a Hot Wheel, and wondering if I'd ever see Dad again.

My cousin Ricky, young in his career, was one of the EMTs that night. I remember tears in his eyes as he worked on his uncle. They mentioned "heart attack." They mentioned "severe." I heard the word "miracle."

We sat in the emergency department for hours. It seemed like days. Finally, a doctor came and talked to us. He said that with the amount of damage, he was very surprised that Dad made it. He mentioned that same word my cousin Ricky had mentioned: *miracle.*

Dad underwent surgery to repair that Sunday night-blown artery. Over the following years, his check engine light came on and they had to open his hood two more times, but it bought him eighteen years. Eighteen more years that many thought he'd never see.

MIRACLE.

So far, I've used that word a lot during this battle.

Messages flood my inbox like I've got free gas coupons. I'm given well-wishes, prayers, and good thoughts. I also get diet tips that slow cancer, including one suggestion for a smoothie made from kudzu and burned motor oil. The sender says it cured her husband's cancer.

"He doesn't even have headaches anymore," she boasts. "It was a miracle!"

Testimonials come in claiming all sorts of things. At least a dozen use the word *miracle,* but one stands out. It comes from a man named Don.

Don tells me he had lung cancer. Doctors claimed they could remove the cancer and start him on chemo. Though it would be a long shot, they said he *may* live another year.

There's that word again, the one doctors throw at us cancer folks: "may."

Don wasn't okay with a "maybe" just to gain a year, so he elected not to go through the torture. Instead, he said he would pray daily. He became fervent in his prayer.

"I didn't pray for God to heal me," he tells me. "I prayed for everybody else going through this to find peace in it. I prayed God would use me for whatever I was still good for. That was it. That was all I asked for. Every day."

He was given one year to live. That was nine years ago. Doctors couldn't explain why each of his scans showed less cancer. They told him he was a living miracle.

Don didn't take to the word too well. He says he'd rather just say that he gave up his body for God to use, and: "Well, I guess He still has a little work left for me."

⸺⸺⸺·•◦∞◦•·⸺⸺⸺

mir·a·cle

/ˈmirək(ə)l/

noun

A surprising and welcome event that is not explicable by natural or scientific laws and is therefore considered to be the work of a divine agency.

THAT's what Merriam-Webster tells me a miracle is. I've got a few different versions.

Miracle: my dad; one who lived a lot longer than his heart did.

Miracle: a man who beat cancer by prayer and offering his body up for the work of the Father.

Miracle: a newborn baby; from conception to the first time oxygen fills the lungs, the entire journey is a miracle created by God.

Miracle: a single parent who learns to juggle work and parenting and still maintains a positive environment.

Miracle: a ninety-year-old lady who still works in her flower garden almost daily. By the way, she lives in my neighborhood and is an absolute blessing to talk to.

Miracle: *YOU!* Yes, you! You are a miracle waiting to happen.

You could be someone else's miracle, like the many reaching out to me. There are people I don't even know offering encouragement. I never knew this ol' boy had so many that cared.

Some tell me I've helped them become a better person through my books and stories. Others thank me for being there for them, recalling tales of how I helped them in rough times. Some say they read their Bible more and have learned to pray more. They say I'm an inspiration. I guess that's just a side effect.

Like Don, I simply want God to use me for His glory. And if y'all get in the way, you have to deal with that yourselves. I also realize all miracles do not happen just because you pray for them.

We have to be obedient and receptive to the stipulations. I learned that at a young age—standing on my porch, clutching a Hot Wheel car as I watched my dad being loaded into the back of an ambulance, not knowing if I'd ever see him again. And I prayed: If God would let my daddy live, I would give up my body and my life for Him to use as He wished. I prayed for a miracle.

Daddy lived. I'm just holding up my end of the bargain.

At least . . . I hope I am.

CAN God use cancer for good things? You tell me.

I've been able to holler about Him from stages, podiums, and the middle of basketball courts. I know He has provided my online audience to grow by leaps and bounds. I use the circumstances to tell others about how Christ can change everything.

Am I good at public speaking? I have a monotone voice, a hillbilly accent, and I often mispronounce words. It probably is not my best option to serve Christ. But if I am given the opportunity to holler for Him, it's game on!

It's all about how strong our faith is and what we actually believe. Do we believe our prayers are heard and dealt with according to His will? Or are we simply hoping that they'll work? Miracles are a product of our believing wholeheartedly that God *will* do what is best for us.

Not long ago, I was in a discussion with a coworker about the survival rate for my cancer. Based on statistics with my diagnosis and progression, it's something some would say I need to pay attention to. Honestly, I don't focus on that. Instead, I put my focus on believing in what God can do with it.

Let me explain . . .

How many of you know the story of Shadrach, Meshach, and Abednego? It's been one of my favorites since I was a kid. Perhaps it's all the names I found interesting. After all, they're so fun to say, but it's also the story itself that left a powerful impression.

The three boys refused to worship an idol despite the king's command. They were bound and thrown into a hot furnace. However, when the king looked in, he saw not only the three boys he'd thrown into the furnace but also a fourth. An angel of God was present with them, and they walked about freely and unbound—without the flames harming them. Because of that miracle, the king then offered praise to their God.

Miracle. . . There's that word again.

I often think about Shadrach, Meshach, and Abednego as I go through this battle against cancer. I find inspiration in how strong their faith was. Their belief in God was immeasurable.

I also find it interesting that God didn't rescue the young boys before they were thrown into the heat. Instead, God showed up with them in the furnace, and they were freed and remained unharmed.

The prayers of Shadrach, Meshach, and Abednego were very powerful. They prayed for God to save them from being thrown into the fire, but even if their God had not saved them in that way, they still refused to serve any false gods. Their faith in His ability to save was great but so was their faithfulness to stay true to God even if He didn't deliver them.

I want my prayers to be like that, too—believing that God can save me. Even if He does not rescue me in the way or timing that I want, I will remain faithful to Him because He is ever-faithful to me.

I know I'm not alone as I battle this evil cuss word. I have felt His presence more than ever as He "shows up in the fire" with me. Perhaps that kind of prayer invites God to work in powerful ways and perform miracles that would not otherwise be possible.

In **John 8:31 (NIV)**, Jesus says:

"If you hold to my teaching, you are really my disciples."

The story of Shadrach, Meshach, and Abednego is a powerful witness to courageously remain in the truth and be a true disciple of Christ, no matter what you're facing. Their faithfulness in truth is what leads them to freedom.

Statistics? Survival rates? I'm not even going to spend a second dwelling on those.

Instead, I will use this time to grow in my walk with Christ and give up my body as a vessel to use as He may. If this leads to a miracle, healing, or even prolonged life, I will be grateful. If not, the reward awaiting me is better than *all* that.

Miracles are seen so differently by people. Some think of them as a gift from God while others don't believe in them at all and say that luck has more to do with it. I have friends who have been products of good luck, which usually involved coupons for burger joints. Miracles are life-changing. They're different, but not everyone can agree on that.

A buddy of mine was grinning ear to ear a few weeks ago. He had every right! The unthinkable happened. Unbelievable even! He told me the story of his miracle:

"Yep! We caught two bass that day. They were too skinny to be sold for fish sticks," he said. "Then, we got on those old bucket mouths back there in them flooded timbers and pulled out the win! If you ask me, it was a miracle."

He hadn't won a fishing tournament since Neil Armstrong left footprints on our neighboring rock, but he did that day. A miracle, not luck. Just ask him!

Perhaps it was. My buddy has always been a believer. He's a third-degree Southern Baptist and has twice won the church chili cook-off.

Jesus sure liked fishermen. And chili. So, maybe. Just maybe.

WHEN I WAS A KID, I believed hard in miracles. All kids do. Especially kids that grow up seeing other kids with things they wished they had. I knew one day, a miracle would show up out of thin air and I'd have a go-cart . . . a vacation at the beach . . . a pet dog that wasn't a recovering stray. I believed in that kinda stuff.

In fact, that's the best part about being a kid. You believe in practically everything. You even believe that when grown people tell you things, they're as true as dogwoods blooming on Easter.

Kids believe in miracles. When your dad hasn't worked in weeks and Christmas is coming up, you still believe in Santa. You just know a Christmas miracle is hanging out, waiting for you to go to bed.

That was me. I was that kid that had the bad habit of believing in everything. Snow in Alabama, sharks in Brilliant Lake, Bigfoot in Fluttering Springs . . . believable stuff. As I grew older, I believed in bigger things.

I believed that Paul William "Bear" Bryant was God's choice for coaching the Crimson Tide. I believed Bo and Luke Duke were my cousins. I also believed Dale "The Intimidator" Earnhardt could see the air. I believed in ghosts, angels, the magic of David Copperfield, and most of all—you guessed it—I believed in miracles.

But something happened.

I grew out of certain things. Things I wished I hadn't. There were changes over the years. I quit believing in stuff. I don't know when it happened, but it did. By fifth grade, I was told I shouldn't believe in notions like Santa, the Tooth Fairy, and name-brand dogs. With that, miracles went out the window.

Humans are hardwired to take the fun out of life. We're hollered at if we believe in things we can't see, but that was hard for me. I still believed in the power of good. I'd seen it firsthand, like the Christmas I spoke of when Dad was out of work.

See, I got a bike that year. It wasn't even second-hand. But it doesn't end there. I got some denim britches: stone-washed kind. Those had *just* been discovered, and *I* got a pair. And more! A collared shirt, socks, and shoes that were just my size.

Dad swore up and down he had no idea where it'd all come from. He didn't have to do much convincing. I already knew. I had prayed for those very things.

We all need that belief. I wish it stayed with us our entire lives. To deny ourselves this human need is like refusing water, nanner puddin', or promising to never fish again.

That Christmas night long ago, I remember sitting in my room with saltwater gathering in my eyes. I thanked God. I didn't pray to Santa. I knew who had made the miracle come true. It was a higher power.

Sometime after I was told to stop all that nonsense, I would sit and wish I still believed like that. I realized I'd let this world steal something beautiful from me. A little piece of my soul. And I didn't understand why I had to stop believing in anything. Especially miracles. I mean, I'm told to believe in the Bible. Well, ain't there miracles in the Bible? Are we not supposed to believe *everything* in there?

First, the number of miracles Jesus performed was sufficient for honest inquirers to believe in them. I've seen drunkards admit to believing in miracles because they're in the Bible.

The four gospels record Jesus performing about thirty-five separate miracles (or thirty-eight depending on what level of deaconship you are). Most of the miracles that Jesus performed are recorded in more than one gospel. Two of His miracles—the feeding of the 5,000 and the resurrection—are found in all four gospels.

I think it was important to list the miracle of the feeding of the masses multiple times. If they hadn't, I'm not sure "dinner on the grounds" would be a thing, and that's important. Fried chicken was invented just for that. Mark noted it. Luke recorded it. John wrote about it. Tax collectors tried to charge him for it. It *must* be true.

Miracles still happen. I've seen desperate men find work. I witnessed a man be delivered from the depths of being an Auburn fan and get anointed by the healing power of Nicholas Lou Saban. I've seen tomatoes grow during droughts. I've watched kids beat cancer. I talked to a guy not long ago who was told he had six months to live. That was eight years ago.

I even once found a baby squirrel that was supposed to die within days. "You'll never be able to keep that thing alive," I was told. I not only raised it until it was big enough to fend on its own, but I taught it not to bite me. At least not all the time.

Folks, miracles happened then, and they can still happen today. It's all about our faith and belief. Miracles are real. As a matter of fact, you may be one.

You can become everything the haters said you'd never be. Everything you ever dreamed of is waiting to happen. Call it whatever you want. You can say it was because of hard work, luck . . . maybe just because of connections you've made. I'd like to believe a miracle played a role in it.

Prove your naysayers wrong. Hug people who once told you to quit believing. To those who hurt you deeply, you can honestly forgive their human shortcomings. You can forgive yourself, too, while you're at it. For not believing in angels, ghosts, and Bigfoot. For not believing in yourself. And most of all, for not believing in miracles. Other people may have told you to stop but it's your fault when you get down to it.

You can believe again. You can become like a kid again. But you can only do such wondrous, spectacular, monumental things if you believe in miracles. I sincerely hope you do because somewhere along the way, you knew they were real, and they should have been the whole time.

On top of the "miracles are just luck" folks, there are the "wish" people. Some say miracles are just wishes that have come true. Nothing more, nothing less. I beg to differ. As children, we wished for big things when we blew out our birthday cake candles, but miracles seem to be much bigger than candle wishes.

Maybe miracles can be associated with the night sky. Perhaps miracles do come from wishes, but they would have to be big wishes.

No—huge wishes. The kinds that come from shooting stars. I've only seen a few of those in my lifetime. Each time, I have been amazed.

Have you ever been mesmerized by the heavens like that? I mean *really* locked in. Not just notice it but truly pay attention to it. The kind of looking that makes your eyes blur after a while. Those are the kind of nights I need right now.

I've been thinking too much about cancer and the "what ifs." Doctors have told me things I don't fully understand. They say things may get worse but may one day be better . . . just not right now. Still, something about looking at the stars makes me worry a little less.

I remember the first time I focused on all those shiny little spots of glitter. It's been forty-something years at least. I was with my friend. We were nine, maybe ten. Big enough to camp out by ourselves all night, at least until 9:00 PM.

He had just buried Bo Duke earlier that day. He bawled until his eyes swelled. Bo Duke was his Beagle. A fine dog he had been—a true best friend. A camping trip would work better than anything at that moment to bring him out of his sadness.

It was a perfect night; not hot or cold. Not a cloud in sight. Overhead were a gazillion stars. It was a beautiful sky, the kind you can only see when you're deep in tractor and pickup territory, almost lost but not quite.

Folks who are used to city lights never believe in a starry sky until they see it for themselves. They gaze up from the middle of a field with no pollution saying things like, "Wow, I can't believe there are that many."

Well, there are. Plus a million. The night I tried to make my buddy forget about Bo Duke, there were even more.

I remember hiking along the creek bank with my friend. He wished Bo Duke were with us. I wished I'd brought more peanut butter crackers.

My friend was over all the crying about Bo Duke, but he was still hurting. He was in that stage where he had cried so much that his eyes had cut him off, and I knew how he felt. I'd already buried a dog and two parakeets by then. I couldn't eat anything for two days after my dog passed (except for candy. Doctor's orders). There comes a moment when you've wept as much as you ever will. My friend was past that. He meant every sniffle and when he couldn't breathe anymore, he stopped.

That night, we were supposed to be doing best-buddy things: building fires, trying to fish, practicing cuss words, making a tent from the quilt Momma gave us. For some reason, we had forgotten how to do any of that. In fact, we just kept walking. Now and then, we would skip a rock or get in a spitting contest. I knew he was sad, so I let him win on purpose. Neither of us talked a whole lot.

We found a clearing along the creek bank and laid out the quilt. We found ourselves laying on our backs. No words. I waited for my pal to talk if he wanted. He didn't. He just stared straight ahead at the night sky.

"Do dogs go to Heaven?" he finally asked.

"Yeah, of course they do."

I made the reply as if I knew what I was talking about. Really, I had no clue, but I didn't want my buddy to think ol' Bo Duke would be worm dirt for the rest of his life.

"I wonder if Bo Duke will remember me when I get there."

"Of course he will," I assured him.

Then it happened.

Something streaked across the sky like a bottle rocket. It seemed so faint against the other stars, but its movement and the trail it left was amazing! I felt something, but I couldn't even describe it. It took me to a place I had never been before. It only lasted a few seconds, then it was gone!

"Shooting star! You see that?!" he hollered.

"I did!" I hollered back, sitting up to watch it disappear into the darkness.

I'd always wondered if shooting stars were real. I'd never seen one in real life, but I had heard that if you saw one, you could make a wish and it would come true. Anything you asked for. *Anything!* No rules, just wish.

"Did you make a wish?" I asked.

"For what?" he responded.

"You're supposed to make a wish, and whatever you wish for will come true," I explained to him with confidence.

"Really?"

"Really!"

He stared back at the sky. His eyes got glossy. He sniffed back snot.

"You okay?" I asked.

"Just wishing," he said.

"For what?" I asked. I'd never seen wishing make anybody cry.

"Something we all need. Every one of us. Maybe even the whole world," he told me.

"Huh? You didn't wish for a bike or nothin'?"

"Nah."

"Well, whatcha wish for?"

"I wished there was less sadness. Burying dogs is hard and being sad is even harder. I don't like it at all. I wish nobody would ever have to cry again. Unless, y'know, they mash their fingers or something," he said in the most serious voice I'd ever heard him use.

I didn't know all the rules for wishing, so I wasn't sure if that was legal or not. Still, I've always wondered if the world had less sadness because of that wish. There's really no way to know. This world could have gone to hell in a handbasket had it not been for that wish. Maybe the sadness we deal with now is ten times less than what it would have been if my buddy hadn't done that for us.

Anyway, I'm just rambling. That was long ago. The rules may have changed since then. I've gotten older and have more things than I could wish for now. I can't remember the last time I was in a spitting contest —it's been months—but I remember everything about that special night. Man, what I would give if making wishes like my buddy's were that easy when you get older.

I think about it and all those stars. I remember how sad my friend was about Bo Duke and how proud he was of his wish. He believed it. I did, too.

I remember how we didn't have a clue how life worked. Many times, it seemed unfair. It's a miracle we made it this far, but I'm not sad anymore. Even dealing with the cuss word inside me; I'm not sad about it.

Maybe it was because of that wish. Maybe wishes work. Maybe they last forever . . . or at least for forty years.

I STILL GO OUT OFTEN and just gaze at the night sky and all those stars. Man, there's a bunch of 'em. I guess the more there are, the higher the chances for one to turn into a wish. I'm always waiting until one breaks loose and runs. I've got a wish waiting on it.

Would I have stood a chance today had it not been for my friend's wish? I wonder . . . And I still wonder if shooting stars and miracles are connected. Is a shooting star a miracle getting thrown down from Heaven?

I know miracles come from Heaven, but where, exactly, is Heaven?

I used to think Heaven was somewhere up there in the middle of galaxies and constellations and episodes of *Star Trek*. I always believed it was a far-off land, like a fairytale kingdom where the only ones allowed inside were those who knew the secret handshake or the password—one like the Little Rascals had at the He-Man Woman Haters clubhouse.

In my simple adolescent brain, Heaven was a huge, dry county filled with Baptist bootleggers. I think somewhere down the line, my dad told me that and I believed it. A Pentecostal might sneak in now and then, but only if they accidentally fell into the baptismal beforehand. At least that's what childhood led me to believe.

To me, both as a kid and now, Heaven is a wonderful place of fishponds and classic rock music. The driveway is protected by mother-of-pearl gates, where security stands before a ledger book and decides who will and won't go to the everlasting cookout.

Everyone in line gets frisked by the security angel until he announces, "Clean!" and then the gates open and you can smell the barbecue.

At one time in my life, Heaven was merely a bunch of clouds and people in bathrobes. I imagined everyone with perfect haircuts and all their teeth. It was kind of like an Abercrombie & Fitch commercial but with no underwear. Heaven was just a bunch of big mansions, or so I thought.

At another time in my life, I even thought that Heaven was just like living down here, with all the same stuff we have right now, like Reese Cups and Grapico—in glass bottles, of course.

But I now know I was wrong about everything concerning God and Heaven. I don't think we'll crave barbecue in Heaven. I think we get served something so wonderful that we forget about pulled pork and brisket. I hope not, but I still think what's up there will be better.

Because it *will* be *so* much better.

Nobody's loved ones die, and there are no doctors or cancer to worry about. Whenever you want a hug, you get it straight from God. He just gives you one, no questions asked. You know, some days, I think I can feel Him practicing on me.

Whatever Heaven is like, I know it will be grand. I know God has made something so wonderful up there that we will be floored. That's why I'm working so hard to get there. No matter what He asks me to do, I am all in. Even public speaking, Lord help us all.

It seems like I'm doing a lot of speaking lately, something I never imagined I'd ever be doing. But God is orchestrating this whole journey, and I'm just along for the ride.

Speaking to crowds scares the living water out of me. It always has.

The first time you ever give a speech to a crowd is truly a special moment, and I will surely never forget the first time I gave a speech. It was horrible. I stumbled over words, forgot my lines, and made a complete fool of myself. People still clapped.

As a kid, I was extremely shy and seldom said anything, choosing to stay quiet most of the time. I'd rather be the kid that went unnoticed than be the one who got attention.

When I was ten, I had a speaking role in our class play with several lines. I went to the teacher and told her I couldn't do it. She told me that she had purposely given me those lines because she knew I could handle it and not screw it up. She even used those words: "screw it up," which I thought was cool coming from a teacher. That teacher also told me she believed in me and if I did it, she would turn my mediocre grade into one that put me on the honor roll.

My first thought was that speaking parts didn't sound like much fun. But hey, who was I to complain if I could get an A so easily? I mean, it couldn't be that much work, could it?

The part was nothing fancy, and I'm sure nobody even remembers it, but the important lesson here is that I got through it, and it taught me something very important: If I was willing to stand up and speak, as frightening as that was, I could do anything to overcome other fears.

Now, I don't know if it was ethical for the teacher to do such a thing. That is a debate for later. My public speaking is still nothing special, but I can now give speeches with confidence.

The truth is, I don't know why anyone would ask me to speak into a microphone at all. I still think I'm horrible at it, but if God puts it in my heart to do something, I will do it with everything in me. Even if my knees shake like Elvis on world tour.

Microphones don't frighten me. It's more the people and the stage.

The first time I ever got on stage, I was maybe eight or so and I sang at our church. At eight years old, you don't realize how horrible your voice is, mainly because mommas are designed to lie to us and tell us how great we sound.

It was a Wednesday night. I was so nervous I puked backstage and ruined the bathrobe that was designated to be Joseph's costume for the Christmas Story play. An older buddy of mine helped me clean up my face. He told me that once I got out there, it would go by quickly.

"Just remember to breathe, or you'll pass out," he told me. He then gave me some sound advice about being on stage: "Imagine the entire audience in their under-britches."

"Do what?!"

"That's right," he went on. "Pretend they're all wearing underwear."

This, he claimed, would take the sting out of my anxiety, and help me remember that everyone is virtually the same beneath the surface.

It sounded like a good idea. It might have worked if the front pews hadn't been filled with members of the women's Bible study group. When I envisioned twenty-one elderly women of virtue in their tighty-whities, I choked and almost puked again.

I was supposed to sing "Silent Night" that Wednesday, but I forgot the words. I ended up singing something from Hank Williams, Jr.'s greatest hits album, and the preacher cut me off thirty seconds into my hollering campaign.

I've been speaking and telling stories for a few years now, but I'm going to admit something to you: I have no idea what I'm doing.

I tell stories of hope, faith, and prayer. I spin tales that are supposed to make people laugh. It's a hit-and-miss kind of job. Sometimes, people laugh. Other times, I find myself in a small country church speaking to folks who I'm not quite certain even have a pulse.

I just don't think I was invented for any of this. I don't think I was meant to do this sort of stuff. In fact, I probably *shouldn't* be doing it. A guy like me is underqualified. Hence, the anxiety. Maybe I should stick to writing misspelled words with bad grammar and overused punctuation.

When I first started, I used to get so nervous—and I'm not proud of this—that my eyes would water when I spoke. Eventually, I got over that bad habit. I rarely get nervous anymore, but a lot of people still remember the old days. I got asked all the time why I cried while telling the story of fishing for bluegills.

To this day, my eyes will sometimes leak. But I'm not scared anymore. I'm changing inside. Maybe I'm starting to grow into my paws, like my mother always said I would. Maybe I'm getting older, or more comfortable in my skin. I don't know. What I *do* know is that nobody expected much out of me. I never expected much from myself, either. But here I am, doing what God asked me to do—and I'm so grateful it hurts.

I'm grateful to still be here. I'm grateful to tell stories about my adventures, my family, and about the words my people say when they stub their toes on wooden coffee tables. I am grateful for my church family and for my friends who believed in an underachieving curly-headed kid from a small town. I'm grateful I don't get as nervous as I used to because what I do is not for me but for my Savior.

It is times like these that God can choose to use us by means we didn't know we were even capable of. When we give our all to Him, sit back, and ask, "How?" instead of, "Why?" then will He show us, and we can look at God at work and be amazed He can use hard times to do something so wonderful. We can choose to recognize that God has the right to use us to reach others, even by taking us through difficult and trying times.

Exodus 14:1-4 (NIV) are some of my favorite verses about this:

> *"Then the LORD said to Moses, "Tell the Israelites to turn back and encamp near Pi Hahiroth, between Migdol and the sea. They are to encamp by the sea, directly opposite Baal Zephon. Pharaoh will think, 'The Israelites are wandering around the land in confusion, hemmed in by the desert.' And I will harden Pharaoh's heart, and he will pursue them. But I will gain glory for myself through Pharaoh and all his army, and the Egyptians will know that I am the LORD." So the Israelites did this."*

God's plan for Israel was not going to be an easy one, but that was the plan Moses was to obey, announce, and lead. Moses was in the difficult predicament of sharing unpopular truths. Believers should get used to it—truth is often inconvenient but always helpful!

Have you ever found yourself in a predicament that scared last night's dinner out of you? We have a lot of word pictures in the English language to describe being in a predicament. We hear phrases such as "you sure have painted yourself into a corner;" caught "between a rock and a hard place;" being "up against the wall;" or "in a pickle."

The events of our lives are not random. God crafted a time and place for us. We tend to forget that when things go wrong.

More often than not, we wonder if we deserve a spanking when things don't go our way. In the face of stern difficulty, we even convince ourselves that the reason we're going through trouble is because of something we've done. It seldom occurs to us that the wilderness and the Sea of Reeds are part of the call of God for us. God has a plan for the troubles!

What about the journey God sent Moses on?

First, God wanted to lure Pharaoh. Sometimes, God uses our lives to pull in the lives of godless men. It is exciting when that purpose is to soften their hearts to see His love and goodness—but that wasn't the case here.

God used the testimony of His people and Moses, their leader, to bring a hardness into Pharaoh that would set him up for judgment. As uncomfortable as that could have been for any of us, our lives are about recognizing God's right to use us for His purposes.

The ultimate endpoint of God's plan was what it always is: to expose who He is to man and the heavenly host. That is His big plan, and we have the opportunity to be used of Him today to do it!

These days, one of the best things about being a born-again believer is the ability to do great things we could never do on our own. We can look around us and see so many others trying to accomplish tasks through their own efforts with varying degrees of success. What gives us such a tremendous advantage, and makes us so successful, is the Holy Spirit working in and through us. Christ empowers us to break down any limitation the world has set up, but only if we let Him.

Voluntarily choosing to enlist God's help allows Him to work miracles that simply aren't possible in the natural realm but are everyday occurrences in the supernatural. For us, this means that Christ helps us reach people that are otherwise unreachable, change minds that seem to be unchangeable, and bring new understanding to people hopelessly confused by the world's way of thinking.

It can be frustrating to watch family, friends, and loved ones who don't understand the Gospel of Grace as they struggle through life; it's normal to want to help them. We can get tired and frustrated if we try through our efforts, but God gives us limitless strength and energy.

"Hast thou not known? hast thou not heard, that the everlasting God, the Lord, the Creator of the ends of the earth, fainteth not, neither is weary? There is no searching of his understanding. He giveth power to the faint; and to them that have no might he increaseth strength. Even the youths shall faint and be weary, and the young men shall

*utterly fall: but they that wait upon the Lord shall renew
their strength; they shall mount up with wings as eagles;
they shall run, and not be weary; and they shall walk, and
not faint."* (Isaiah 40:28-31 KJV)

During His earthly ministry, Jesus healed the sick and the lame, restored sight to the blind, and even brought the dead back to life. He has given us the power to do this and much more.

---

*"Verily, verily, I say unto you, He that believeth on me, the
works that I do shall he do also; and greater works than
these shall he do . . ."* (John 14:12 KJV)

God has a definite agenda for the good things He wants to do in our lives and in the world, and enlisting His help allows us to be His hands and feet.

Trusting Him to work through us gives us perfect ideas and strategies that don't come from us but from a higher source. Whether it makes sense to our logical minds at the time is beside the point; we simply need to believe that He wants the best for us. Allowing Him to be our ally is always our best course of action.

Sometimes, we just have to get out of the way and say, "Okay, God. I am nothing but a puppet, and you are the Puppet Master. Use me for your will."

When that time comes, simply stand amazed at what happens. Just look at God!

CHAPTER 12

WHEN WILL IT END?

Cancer will steal everything that you let it. It will take away things from you that used to be commonplace. However, there are things you can stand your ground on: your smile, your happiness, and your desire to make every day meaningful.

There are also a few things that are out of your control, like your energy and stamina. Those things get zapped by treatments and the body's natural defense of fighting back.

Out of everything you can't control, time is the one that affects me most. It seems I never have enough time to do what needs to be done. I'm either at appointments or recovering from treatments. Time just seems to be out of control when it comes to fighting cancer.

You count the weeks and days until your next appointment and make note of every ache and pain, thinking it might be a signal of your disease worsening. On the day of your appointment, you're so anxious that you arrive at your physician's office early only to discover he's behind schedule, increasing your waiting time as well as your apprehension. During your visit, your physician orders the required tests and tells you to go home and wait for a phone call—or suggests you call back in a few days or a week to get your test results.

You are always waiting for something: the initial diagnosis following surgery; a biopsy, scans, or fine needle aspiration; the results of a treatment, or your next checkup. Waiting becomes your new hobby.

The most difficult aspect of waiting is the open-ended uncertainty of not knowing what's happening inside your body. Conversely, knowing can be a relief—even when the news is not good—because you and your physician can then take action and discuss therapeutic alternatives.

You should also be aware that the time you spend waiting for appointments and information on your medical status is often determined by circumstances beyond your control or that of your physician. Still, you want someone to blame for all the time you sit and drain your phone battery reading the gossip on Facebook. But who?

The ones you think you should blame are most often not the ones at fault.

For example, because of economic pressures, most physicians see more people per hour today than they saw in the past, resulting in shorter office visits. This can make you feel like your psychosocial needs received insufficient consideration. Physicians' increasingly heavy workloads also lead to longer patient appointment waiting periods, whether for an initial consultation or subsequent therapy.

We spend more time getting to know strangers in waiting rooms than we do with the doctor that will direct our healing. I have been invited to cookouts, baby showers, and bar mitzvahs while waiting to put my deductibles to use.

In short, facing delays is a part of the treatment of cancer. Waiting is part of the grand design, or so it seems. We are waiting on all sorts of things: waiting for a nurse to arrive to draw blood; waiting for a courier to pick up blood; waiting for another courier to drop off chemotherapy drugs; waiting for a nurse to arrive to connect the infusion pump and then later waiting again for another nurse to disconnect it.

I spend lots of time waiting for my name to be called for scans. Then I wait with my doctor while another specialist reads the scans and reports to the oncologist, who then finally delivers the news to me. Then we all wait to see what a panel of other oncologists thinks will be best for me and their attempt to retire early and buy more BMWs.

Seemingly short appointments turn into full-day affairs for

patients and their care partners. We have to take a day off from work, and we can't plan anything else around it. We must be at the doctor's office at sunrise so we can wait all day. We miss events and lunches, and our coupons expire while we wait. Waiting has never been my strong point, so it's worse than using my fishing money to pay deductibles.

Don't get me wrong. It all sucks. Waiting is just a byproduct of sucking.

Having a port in your chest sucks. Simple things like putting on a shirt pull and tug at the port. Bumping it sucks. Backpacks have to be carefully placed. Car seatbelts are the devil.

Fatigue sucks, too. It's never-ending. Your appetite is constantly changing. But waiting? Waiting is like something being stolen from you that you will never get back.

When I first received a phone call from a patient case worker at Memorial Sloan Kettering Cancer Center in New York City, I had no idea what I would be dealing with, but I knew waiting was in the formula. One of the first things I was told was that there would be several tests and procedures to make sure I was a candidate. I knew that meant more waiting and more uncertainty.

Once I found out I was accepted, I was told that in order to do the trial, I would be administered very low doses of chemotherapy. I had been reluctant to do chemotherapy, which is why I was steered toward immunotherapy.

I wasn't sure how I felt about the news. Initially, I was reticent. I didn't know enough about it to ask questions or give opinions, so I asked if chemo was absolutely necessary. I will never, ever forget what she told me.

She said, "I'm trying to save your life. We can do this or not do this, but I think we should try it."

That was a direct statement. It got my attention. I had spent so much time "waiting" that I forgot my life was at stake and ultimately, staying above the dirt was my goal, no matter what. I put my head down right there and prayed about it.

The first time I looked up the disease online, I read that it had a high mortality rate; I know how aggressive cancer can be once it's in the lymph nodes. I decided I didn't need any more time to consider. I printed the paperwork that was emailed to me and signed it right then.

I still didn't know for sure what "low-dose chemo" was, so I began asking questions. Doctors in New York learned quickly they had to dumb it down for this old country boy. They said it would be given on top of my immunotherapy; one would help the other.

"You can think of these two medications like Pepsi and Coke," my trial doctor told me. "They're both given intravenously through your port, and both are pretty much the same."

At first, I thought the treatment would be much more involved. I thought maybe the IV treatment would be like dialysis, what I imagine is like being tied to a machine and your whole life centers around that. But this treatment is very different. It's almost like taking a vitamin shot every few weeks.

The medical team is careful to monitor me every step of the way. The general process and amount of care are almost overboard in terms of making sure everything is okay, but it's comforting.

When I started the first chemo treatment, enough doctors and nurses surrounded me to start my own co-ed softball team. They made me feel at ease about something I was terrified of. The immunotherapy going through my veins created a tickling sensation. I worried about that, too, and I thought it might be the beginning of an adverse reaction. It wasn't, but all kinds of things went through my mind. Having a team that asks those questions—"What's going on? Anything new? Any rashes? Are you feeling sick?"—was reassuring and continues to be.

Luckily, I didn't experience any serious side effects from the treatment. Aches and pains are present. Nausea is here. Those things are part of my life now. Nothing new. My most common side effects are fatigue and flu-like symptoms because the treatment has activated my immune system to fight the cancer.

Some patients deal with tougher side effects that often seem like those experienced by people going through chemotherapy, including hair and weight loss. The only difference is when people get chemotherapy, they expect to feel bad for a few days or weeks after the treatments, then they feel better. With immunotherapy, the serious side effects can start weeks or even months after the treatment.

I was initially told that, according to statistics, I had an estimated year and a half to live. I never believed that.

In the very beginning, I thought my cancer had the potential to be a death sentence, but I also had faith that God was already working on my behalf. I expect to be here for a while. The future is bright for me and other people diagnosed with the disease. I feel it. The advances are coming, and all the credit goes to the people who wake up every day and make it their goal to help people like me get well.

These trials taking place are just for that reason. Even if they don't work for me, it still means we're one step closer to getting it right for others. These doctors are amazing, and they are giving it their all.

My family and friends are behind me. Having a strong support group, people who care about you, is invaluable. It gives me the strength to go through anything.

I know I want to live, but the battle is a tough one. Some days, I feel defeated. It takes the people who love you to bring you back out again. They give me so much strength.

And while they support me, they also wait. Waiting is part of this, and it is something every cancer patient has to accept.

We wait for answers, and we wait for victory. In the middle of all the waits, we make decisions that affect our lives. Thankfully, the decision-making part is something I have always embraced.

I WAS RECENTLY ASKED for my opinion about an important decision.

A friend asked me, "Russell . . ." and I knew he was talking to me because people had been calling me that all day.

"Russell, I just don't know which way to go. What would you do?"

The question was about a business he owned. He had a great opportunity to close his shop and go to work for another owner on a larger scale. Less stress. Paid insurance. A retirement plan. It seemed like an easy decision.

"It's just that owning this business was my dream. The money would be better there, but I feel like I would be giving up on something I prayed so hard for," he explained.

Decisions, decisions—if they were easier, nervous pills would have never been invented.

Decisions like my friend's are some we get emotionally involved in. My answer may not fit his need because I hadn't realized the dream of owning my own business as he had.

Another example:

I talked to my buddy, Drew, not long ago about the "what ifs" regarding my cancer battle. It was before I knew I was accepted into the New York trial with new treatments. I had no idea that what we would talk about would be so vital in just a few short weeks.

"What if the doctors want to change my treatment to chemo? If this stuff keeps spreading, I know that's what they'll want to do," I asked him.

He replied, "Pray about it."

"I did. Over and over. I feel like God led me to do immunotherapy. If I bail out now and change to chemo, is that not giving up on what God led me to? Is that not short-changing my faith?"

Drew went on to give me several examples from the Bible where God changed directions for His followers. He explained that God is *always* working on our behalf and will give us wisdom to know when and where He is calling us. Drew explained that sometimes God takes us through things because He has prepared a lesson made just for us.

When God calls us to the base of the impossible mountain, he completely means for us to climb it. He's there with us the entire way. He doesn't expect us to do it by our own strength but to lean into His. Once we get to the top, we will see what He wants to show us, and we will never be disappointed.

God has never called me to the base of a mountain that, when I finally reached the top, I didn't stand in awe of what I was seeing on the other side.

ANOTHER GOOD FRIEND ONCE PONDERED "WHY" during a tough time.

As his son clung to life, he whispered to himself, "There's got to be something beautiful on the other side of this moment."

He admits, he doesn't know where it came from, but he now understands what it meant.

My friend watched as his son ran to Jesus. He would not let the end of his child's battle be the end of what all could be accomplished by his short life. He and his wife now host events throughout the year to help folks, mainly children, with expenses associated with battling cancer.

They were at their mountain. They climbed it. God held their hands. He pulled them to the next step when they were so broken, they couldn't reach for it. And together, they stood on the peak.

What they saw on the other side was nothing short of beautiful. They climbed the mountain. They let their decision be made with prayer and faith.

Unfortunately, all too often, our flesh-laden idols prevent us from ever setting foot on the trail that leads up our mountains. It comes through in a desire to do nothing but preserve what we are comfortable with rather than press forward and grow. It's about *our* purpose and *our* plan—not God's.

How do we weather seasons in life when big decisions have to be made? How do we stay focused when we bury loved ones or change jobs, when we're storm-tossed at sea, or when everything we need has been stripped away?

You lose your job. You're bombing several classes. Your home feels like a battleground. You've just been diagnosed with a serious illness. Your church is in dire straits . . . In these seasons, many of us (myself included) feel like we need something new—a new Word from God that applies directly to our situation.

In the crazy storms, the shipwrecks, the starless nights and sunless days, we don't know how God will save us. But we do have His promises. And when we get to the end of our lives, we will be able to say, "I had no idea how He would save me or how I would make it to the end, but never once did He fail to keep His promise."

What about the mustard seed? The parable of the mustard seed in **Matthew 13:31-32** reminds us that all we need is the slightest amount of faith. Even the smallest things can turn into the greatest blessings.

We know that our faith can move mountains, but sometimes, God doesn't see fit to move that mountain. He wants us to grow in Him. He wants us to develop a stronger relationship during the trial we're up against. He wants us to climb the mountain.

I'm currently climbing a mountain. God hasn't removed my cancer, so I'm climbing.

Sure, He has the power to take every ounce of it away: the tumors, surgeries, financial woes, the worry. All of it. But He hasn't. Instead, He's reached down, grabbed my hand, and said, "Let's do this."

And I've never felt closer to Him.

It may be hard to comprehend what I'm about to say, but maybe I need this. Maybe this cancer is what I need to push through to reach the next level in my relationship with Christ. Maybe I need a mountain to climb just so I can see the beauty on the other side.

Don't be discouraged if things don't go your way. Don't give up and think God hasn't answered your prayers. This may be when He wants to show you something so grand that the only way He can is for you to do it together.

When your mountain won't move, don't wait for something to happen. Go over it!

You have to first be willing to make that decision. You can curl up in a fetal position or stand tall and start climbing. The waiting game is going to be part of it, but you must learn that there are things to enjoy even while you wait.

I've met a lot of people during my waits. Most come from lobby waiting rooms and trips to my New York treatments. One such chance encounter came from a gentleman I'll never forget. It wasn't so much the man himself but the question he asked me.

"Whaddya in for?"

It startled me. I was fully engaged in scrolling through alien conspiracies and tailgate recipes on the great source of knowledge known as Facebook.

His question sounded more like something heard on Cell Block C, but where we were was nowhere near that. It was way worse.

Cancer is always the topic of discussion at the treatment center. The place stays full of bald heads and insurance deductibles. It's where all of us come when we're going through a living hell. That day, the awful smell of disinfectant lingered everywhere.

I put down my phone and looked up. He was an approved six feet away, sitting in a chair that swallowed him. He was frail. His button-up shirt was three sizes too big. It probably fit perfectly just a few trips ago.

"Pre-op appointment," I answered. "They're gonna unzip me again this Friday."

"Cancer?" he asked.

"Yep."

"The bad kind?"

"Is there any other?"

"What are they calling yours?" he quizzed me.

"Take your pick," I told him. "Melanoma started all this mess. It got mad and attacked my lymph nodes. Had a surgery or four. Been doing treatments. Popped up in my kidney now. Left side. They say this one is renal cell carcinoma. More lymph nodes coming out with it."

He shook his head. "Dang it, son. You a show-off, ain't ya?"

"Go big or go home!" I replied through a smile. "What about you? What'd they sentence you for?"

"They got me with neuroblastoma. Caught red-handed."

I had to Google it . . . and good grief! If you don't know what that is, think: the worst cancer imaginable. Then triple it. Then multiply it by sheer terror. Carry the two. Divide by financial crippling. That's *before* it gets bad.

His treatment folder read like an unabridged Chinese dictionary. A port drilled in his chest, four rounds of chemo, invasive surgery, radiation, months of immunotherapy, scans, so much blood work he couldn't hold water. Like I said—a living hell.

He shifted himself, obviously fighting pain. "They've been cutting on me since Day One. Almost haven't got anything left to take." He paused to point to his narrow face. His smile was so big I had to squint from the glare. "But they can't take this away."

I could relate. I'd been using my smile as well and trying to hold on to it for months.

See, some days it's forced but I always feel better afterwards. Let me explain:

I haven't had a good night's sleep in a month of Sundays. It seems like I'm at one of the UAB campuses more than I'm at home. Doing anything tires me out. I have to take a nap if I laugh too hard. I get so worked up that all I have left that works right are my cheek muscles, so I use them to smile, and I do it often. I guess I'm afraid it will one day fail me, too. So, I'm using it while I can.

It's been hard. I won't sugarcoat it. Some days are worse than others.

Don't get me wrong. Every day is a blessing. I absolutely love life. If I weren't walking with God, having cancer would be like bench-pressing a cement truck. Still, having two kids makes things even harder. Trying to tell them as much as you can without their world falling apart? That's tough.

My children know everything, but I don't want them to realize what's happening. I worry more about them and my wife than I do myself. They're the ones that are affected. It's like secondhand cancer.

As I sat waiting on my name to get called so they could swipe the paint off my debit card, I realized I don't have it so bad. There are folks way worse than me.

Waiting with us were kids with bald heads. I watched a little girl play with her Barbie, and Barbie's head was bald, too. One boy wore a Spider-Man costume—the whole thing: socks, mask, everything! Complete with a web shooter.

I watched as I waited, mesmerized by kids with smiles and mommas without. Another little girl sat in her mom's lap. She was too scared to move. A boy, maybe ten at the most, had on a baseball cap. I imagined he loved playing baseball. I bet he was great . . . when he could play. Cancer robbed that from him.

Spider-Man made noises that—I guess?—a web shooter makes. He hit everybody in the waiting area with make-believe webs. I got nailed. Twice!

I smiled at Spidey. He smiled back. I couldn't see his mouth, but his eyes smiled so hard his face might have stuck like that.

Those eyes . . .

Those little, hopeful eyes.

They did something to me, did something to *my* eyes. They fogged up like I had top-shelf cataracts. Then the dam broke. My emotions ran down my face and soaked my germ mask.

I had a pocket full of "God Is Bigger" bracelets. I take them with me everywhere. That day, they all got one. Everyone in the room! Mommas and daddies included. Spidey got two.

It's just not fair, dadgummit.

I've done some crappy things in my life. I took every tag off every mattress I've ever owned. I've driven seventy in a fifty-five and cheated in algebra class. I eat fried foods and tell my doctor I have no idea why my cholesterol is up.

I don't like this terrible thing, but I understand why I got this cuss word growing in me. I guess it's payback for all the things I didn't do right. But kids, they haven't even had a chance to screw up. Regardless, forty-seven kids in the United States are diagnosed with cancer every day.

I looked it up. Sitting right there that day, getting hit by invisible spiderwebs, I saw the statistics. That's approximately 17,000 kids each year. How's that fair?

The good news is that 84 percent of those kids will be cured. The bad news is you never know for certain whether *your* kid will be in that 84 percent.

You can't relax. Twenty-four hours per day, you're afraid. You learn never to trust good news; you learn to never—NEVER—get your hopes up. Prayer is your full-time job. But somehow, some way, you can *always* smile.

Look, I'm good with my diagnosis. I'm perfectly okay with it. I found peace in a place where it should be extinct.

Doctors told me to get ready for a long, rough ride. I told them to get ready for a great big miracle. I'm in this for something bigger than myself. It's bigger than just beating the stew out of this cuss word. It's about Him. It's about my God.

I have said before: I didn't "get cancer." Instead, God "ALLOWED me to use cancer" to glorify Him. I wouldn't say I was chosen for this, but I will take the job. I'm trying like my life depends on it, because . . . Well.

I could say at the end of this, when I beat it, that I will have a humdinger of a testimony. That may be the case. But why wait? Why can't I use this struggle to tell others about how great God is now? What's wrong with shouting from the rooftops today?

It's easy to shout glory to Him after you've beat cancer. It's easy to talk about great things when things are, you know, going great.

I want to stand in the fire, laugh in the devil's face, and sing God's praises. I want to tell others about how great He has been to me all while hooked up to chemicals that glow and cause me to hurt all over. What He endured for me can't even be compared to how little I can do for Him.

On the days that I hurt really bad . . .

On the days I feel defeated . . .

On the days that rank right up there next to getting hit by a full-grown garbage truck, I want to smile and tell others that God *is* bigger.

A skinny little man fighting for his life smiled at me that day and told me that nothing or nobody could take his smile. I gave him one of my bracelets and told him that God wouldn't let them if they tried. I wished like the dickens he'd ask me that question again: "Whaddya in or?"

I'd have a different answer now that I've had a chance to think about it. It's rather simple.

I would tell him, "I'm in it for God."

Experiences like that are something I never would have gotten had I not been waiting. That doesn't mean I like waiting, but it means if I must, I will get something from it.

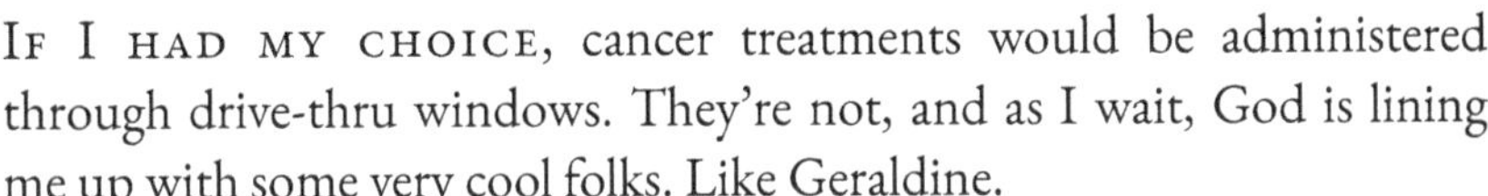

IF I HAD MY CHOICE, cancer treatments would be administered through drive-thru windows. They're not, and as I wait, God is lining me up with some very cool folks. Like Geraldine.

She's my new friend that lives in the Big Apple. I *knew* I could make friends there, but I still feel bad it took nearly six hours to do so.

Geraldine makes the world's best red velvet cake. She told me that herself, and as long as I've known Geraldine, she's never lied to me.

It was early in the morning when I met her. She heard me asking the hotel concierge where the best cup of coffee could be found nearby.

"Your accent . . . You from way down south, yes?" she asked.

"Alabama," I confirmed, showing all my teeth.

"I knew it," she said as she left her cleaning cart and came closer. "I grew up next door: Mississippi."

"You're my cousin!" I hollered.

She automatically qualified for a hug. She got one.

Geraldine's story is amazing . . .

It was 1988, and Mississippi had nothing to offer an eighteen-year-old with the fire and determination Geraldine had trapped inside her. Some weekends, late at night, she found clips from Broadway on her cable television. She watched until she fell asleep. Geraldine had never been to the Big Apple, but she dreamed of it. She even had an aunt who worked in the New York Public Library.

Her small high school didn't offer any kind of drama club, acting lessons, or glee cults. Though she knew her purpose on Earth was to entertain and make people smile, her little school and town offered no escape route. There were auto mechanics and boxing at the gravel pit. That was it.

Geraldine sang at her Baptist church. When she could grab a solo, she owned it! She hollered, stomped, and ran so much that she almost got reprimanded by the head deacon and two ushers. Geraldine had way more to offer than the ancient pages of a hymnal. So, she took a chance. She hopped a Greyhound to New York and moved in with her aunt.

Once settled, she worked at restaurants and convenience stores. She tried out for every show within earshot of the Brooklyn Bridge. She soon grabbed a few background spots but nothing that quenched her thirst.

Then, a new show premiered on Broadway, one that was supposed to be the best thing since King Kong hung off the side of the Empire State Building. Geraldine went for it and snagged a role. It wasn't a lead, but it wasn't background. She was dancing and hollering onstage like Aretha Franklin.

By year two, things were going great. Geraldine had a spot on lockdown and was gaining steam. She met a male lead that swooned her like a teenage boy with his first truck. That's when things changed.

Geraldine was "with child," but her boyfriend wasn't. He bolted like he had a warrant.

Complications ensued. The baby was killing her. Doctors said she should abort. Even if she lived, her baby would not. Geraldine said she would die first before taking a baby the Good Lord gave her. Everyone waited to see which came first.

That was many moons ago.

Geraldine no longer lives with her aunt. She's now fifty-two years young and cleans the rooms where I stayed. She's never been married— only dated two other men in the last three decades.

She still routinely attends Broadway plays and sings at Madison Avenue Baptist Church in Manhattan. She invited me to visit. I told her I would be back monthly. I promised I'd accept the invite but only if she had a solo hollering part and red velvet cake afterward.

That day, we sat on a bench in the hotel lobby and talked about life. We discussed God and how His plans usually don't align with ours, but when we trust Him, we learn to be happy with what He gives us.

I gave Geraldine one of my wristbands. She gave me something I didn't know I was looking for. Assurance.

God led me to New York. I wasn't sure if it was the right place or not. I wasn't positive if I had sought out this new cancer treatment or if God led me to it.

Geraldine told me how she has led many young ladies to Christ. Most of those young women worked with her at the hotel, the same hotel she never would have worked at if Broadway had worked out. She followed Him. His role for her was much more important than anything she could have grabbed on stage. And she's happy.

Oh, and that baby that almost killed her?

That baby made it. That baby isn't a baby anymore. She works on Broadway as a makeup artist.

The show that Geraldine nailed a part in back in '88 was *Phantom of the Opera*—the longest-running show on Broadway. It's the very show her daughter works on.

God sure has a way of blessing us when we follow Him. Geraldine smiles like a possum eating a sweet tater every time she attends the show.

As for me, I have a new friend. I gave her at least a dozen more little bands to hand out.

"Got two new girls I'm working on," she told me. "They are almost ready. I can just feel it!"

I think I'll keep doing what I can to spread God's love to anyone that takes time to listen. I'm not sure what my future holds but blessed assurance is part of it. I didn't tell Geraldine about my cancer. Our talk was going too well to ruin it.

"So, what brings you to New York?" she asked.

I just smiled. "Like you, it was just something inside me."

GERALDINE WAS SUCH a blessing to me. I don't know why I write about random folks I meet. I'm drawn to them in random places.

Folks who are down on their luck. Folks who grew up learning to work harder than a V6 pulling a homecoming float full of the entire junior class. People that, at one time, would save S&H Green Stamps all year just to buy cast-iron pans. I don't know why, but those seem like my people.

Maybe I relate to them. Maybe I see a lot of myself in them. Maybe it's because I recognize tired eyes that tell good stories. Eyes that, if I looked far enough into, I'd recognize "home."

I don't have a clue why a nobody like me writes about people who just want to buy groceries and go home, or perhaps do a good deed unnoticed. Maybe they only want to have lunch with me, and, for some reason, I pull a whole story out between chews of meatloaf and okra.

It may be a curse, but I see intentions. Good intentions. Those worth telling you about. When I talk to people that have more to tell than what they can, I let them pull over and I drive from there. None of these people make headlines. Most don't have titles after their names or have ever taken home a major award. If you look back through my stories, you would be hard-pressed to find someone who wrote a hit song, discovered a breakthrough drug, or organized any earth-shattering movements.

So, I don't have an answer for you except to say that sometimes I am so proud to be a part of regular people, I just feel like saying it. I've never been more than regular and sometimes, people like us go unnoticed. I notice them, then I make sure you do, too. I want to write awful collections of poor sentence structures about them . . .

People like Alan. I met him on a job site, and we instantly became cousins.

He once drove over an hour out of his way to bring me a jar of homemade sauerkraut. Then he spent another hour with me just talking. We talked about gardens, construction, and Alabama football. We even talked about why he hadn't been fishing in weeks.

"There's a litter of kittens in the boat," he said. "Ol' momma cat must feel safe there."

I've eaten green beans from Alan's garden. I've had mater sammiches from a brown paper sack with him. I told him about my secret fishing place on Lake Nicol. He agreed not to share it and didn't even cross his fingers when he promised.

Alan may never have his name in lights. He may never dine with Saint Nicholas Lou Saban, Jr. But Alan is as much like me as my own blood. He works hard and cares harder. He's good people.

Then there's Helen. She's nothing special if you ask her.

I beg to differ.

Helen is a retired schoolteacher who spends her spare time visiting nursing homes where she gives away her crocheted creations. She spends hours making what, to many, may look like something made by nine-year-olds in a VBS class, but the little old ladies down at the home love them, and that makes them as valuable as a Picasso.

I met Helen when my mom was in hospice care. She made my mother the most beautiful Alabama drink koozie. It had an elephant on it. Mom thought it was a dog. I never told her any different. She loved her dog koozie.

I ran into Helen at a grocery store not long ago. We discussed the price of American-made potatoes. I told her I still had that drink koozie. She told me she still makes them. In fact, she pulled one from her purse and gave it to me.

"On the house," she said. "Don't even have to be in the nursing home. You're grandfathered in."

It was much appreciated; the koozie and the fact I didn't have to be in a nursing home to gain ownership.

Helen may never appear in a magazine or on a news story, but she's caused more smiles than homemade cobbler. She's my kind of people.

Have I ever told you about my friend, Marty?

Marty is a roofer by day. In the evenings, he likes to eat fried bologna and sit on his porch and write. He's responsible for songs, stories, poems, and even jokes that cause daily Facebook reviews.

I once told him, "Marty, you should publish some of these stories. Write a book. You have a gift."

In his "aww, shucks" personality, he replied, "Y'know, I just enjoy it. I'm not worried about being published. If I can make folks smile, feel good, and recall nice memories, well, I'm just fine with that."

Marty has worked hard his entire life, been a great friend, and was always one of the first to call me when things weren't going my way. He thinks of others before himself. He's honest, trustworthy, and caring.

He may never see a book with his name on it in the Walmart, but to me, he's a bestseller. In fact, he is to many folks. His writing makes people stop and think. It helps them escape from the living hells they encounter daily.

I still don't know exactly why I'm attracted to these folks like a moth to a flame, a bird to a worm, a tornado to a trailer park. But that's not the point. What I'm getting at is *why?*

Why all this kind-hearted, feel-good, caring about others? What's it all about?

The reason I ask is that all the compassionate people you encounter aren't just random folks like they think they are. These are your lifelong friends. Your mechanics. Your coworkers.

You may be one of these people yourself. Perhaps you don't even know it.

They are folks that leave work boots at front doors. Wear overalls. Bake banana nut bread for a neighbor because it cures bad news.

Sometimes, it's too easy to look over these folks because noticing the "bad" in this world is easy. The talking heads on TV get paid good money to scream garbage at us every single day. It's just simpler to focus on sadness. It's more convenient to see unfairness, injustice, and remind us of country music bands that wear skinny jeans and sound more like hip-hop than anything ever approved by the Grand Ole Opry.

Every now and then, the news does talk about good things. They'll show someone wearing a tailor-made suit; they're smiling because they just wrote a $25,000 check that will go to build a $300 "take a book-leave a book" library box. Smiling is easy when you're spending taxpayer money on stuff like that.

There are times that I begin to have doubts about our species. I wonder how many are still in it for the right reasons. I have some doubts if charities are even charitable. I lose my way at times. Then, people like Alan, Helen, and Marty come along. Smiling. Driving over an hour out of their way just to check on me. Doing things to bring smiles.

These people simply keep their heads down and aid others. They couldn't care less about the recognition. They help others get through rough times like I'm in now. They show up while I wait. They spend their money and time making sure people feel better today than they did yesterday. They help us when we need it—mend things, heal things, grow things, build things, and love things.

Why do I write about these ordinary folks?

Well, to me, they are extraordinary. They're some of the best folks God ever offered us. I think they deserve more than what this mediocre writer can offer but it's the best I can do.

They're there in the waiting periods when you're looking for any reason in the world to find a reason to smile. I want to remind everyone that it's folks like this who make this world a good place. Ordinary people. Good people. People that are worth way more than they'll ever know.

So, no; you might not be changing the entire world. But if you ask me, you're showing the world where a good starting place is.

AND TO THINK, all these people I meet lead me to stories I write. God even provides a stage or microphone from which I get to holler about these people. I get to use the situations placed before me to tell others about how unique we are.

I remember one occasion when I was getting ready to go onstage, and I was a nervous wreck. I'm in a comfort zone around people. People make me smile. So, why I was nervous, I do not know.

It was only minutes until I took the stage. I was being introduced. I wanted to rehearse my thoughts off-stage, but I was caught up in more important things instead, like hoping I wouldn't stink. Is that what all speakers think about before they go onstage? Is it just me?

I always say a silent prayer that goes, more or less, the same way: "Dear God, don't let me look like a complete idiot."

I have come to the conclusion that I will be, at least, a partial idiot, but if I can save myself from "complete idiot" status, it will be a good night.

You'd think that if all you're doing is telling stories, there's not much you can screw up. After all, they're your stories so nobody knows whether you got it right. But it is much harder. Trust me. I've learned to screw up things toddlers could master.

In fact, it's very easy to stink at storytelling because there are no rules. When something doesn't have rules, people like me take advantage and prove to everyone that rules are needed.

I have no idea how or why God led me to use storytelling as part of my tribute to Him through battling cancer. I've never been a storyteller.

A story writer? Perhaps. But telling? Zilch! The only training I had was listening to uncles and older cousins tell lies from front porches at family reunions.

When I think about it, I wouldn't want anyone else to train me but old men in polyester britches so high they stained their trousers with deodorant. I've always had an old soul. I have been an old man since the age of ten. What I most liked about them was they let go of any worry of being embarrassed. They didn't care if their clothes were in style or whether they'd had a haircut in the last six months.

That was me in a nutshell. My clothes were hand-me-downs. I got haircuts anytime we got money back on tax returns. I'd basically followed all the rules for AARP membership by the time I got my first pimple.

I never knew either of my grandfathers. They bought land in Heaven and planted a garden before I was born. I looked for anyone with white hair that would pay attention to me, so I picked up a lot of their traits. Talking just so happened to be one I enjoyed the most.

Maybe that's how I started telling stories—because my life was spent in the company of old men who loved to tell them. Most of the porches I sat on were so full of overalls and scruffy beards that a story always broke out. They just could not restrain themselves from telling stories if their hunting dog's life depended on it.

Old men in overalls are different from your modern-day stockbrokers and business suit guys. They don't have big ambitions (if any). They've outgrown all that. Most did so, like me, by age ten. They're ready to integrate what they know into the world around them. If you listen, they will help you. They tell stories that change your life, make you laugh, and make you grow bigger tomatoes. They do so because they have experiences they want to share.

After all, old men have seen their mistakes get worse over time and watched their qualities get better with age. They've lost those they care about and discovered success is nothing. Simple evenings spent in the shade are worth more to them than a crowded beach or cruise ship.

Sure, they're grumpy at times. They may get too involved in the unapproved Baptist moonshine. Sometimes, their backs go out. But they're honest. They will tell you like it is. No sugarcoating.

Other times, they'll say something so amazing, so incredibly put that you have to write it down and tell people about it the next time a microphone is handed to you. They are filled to the deodorant-stained waistbands with stories. If you listen carefully, they'll tell you one while eating apple slices from a pocketknife.

These men are a dying breed. When they're gone, you will miss the H-E-Double-Hockey-Sticks out of them.

So, I guess the Good Lord has bestowed upon me the gift of gab that comes from ancient front porches. The only way for me to come up with stories worth a hill of beans is to keep going to these appointments, where I wait.

While I wait, I'll talk to strangers. I will pass out little wristbands. I will write about the people I meet and share those stories from the front porch of Facebook.

If I'm telling the correct tales, the ones that tell others of God's love . . . Well, I guess He'll let me keep telling them.

CHAPTER 13

FAITH OR FEAR

Cancer is scary. It can be downright horrifying. It can take your health, your job, and your finances. That's *if* you're lucky. For the unlucky, cancer can take a life.

You get so worked up over fearing your life will soon end that you depress yourself into a never-ending cycle of sleeping and watching cable television. Fear can consume you. But that's where faith comes in.

If you don't understand what true faith is, you can never experience its blessings. So, what is the true meaning of faith?

The closest the Bible comes to offering an exact definition is **Hebrews 11:1 (ESV):**

> ***"Now faith is the assurance of things hoped for, the conviction of things not seen."***

From this particular passage, we see that the central feature of faith is confidence or trust. In the Bible, the object of faith is God and His promises.

Faith is *more* than intellectual agreement.

"Whaddya mean, Russell?"

167

I know, I know! This stuff is hard to get straight. Let me paint you a picture and tell you a story.

To use an old illustration, imagine you're at Niagara Falls, watching a tightrope walker push a wheelbarrow across a rope high above the falls. After watching him go back and forth several times, he asks for a volunteer to sit in the wheelbarrow as he pushes it across the falls.

At an intellectual level, you may believe that he can successfully push you across the rope and over the falls, but you're not exercising Biblical faith until you *get in* the wheelbarrow and *entrust* yourself to the tightrope walker.

Genuine Biblical faith expresses itself in everyday life. In **James 2:17**, the Apostle James tells us that faith by itself, apart from works, is dead. Faith works through love to produce tangible evidence of its existence in a person's life, just as **Galatians 5:6** tells us.

Put another way, the obedience that pleases God comes from faith rather than a mere sense of duty or obligation. There is all the difference in the world between the husband who buys his wife flowers out of delight and the one who buys them simply out of duty.

Faith is so important because it is the means by which we have a relationship with God:

"For by grace you have been saved through faith."
(Ephesians 2:8 ESV)

Faith is how we receive the benefits of what Jesus has done for us. He lived a life of perfect obedience to God, died to pay the penalty for our sinful rebellion against God, and rose from the dead to defeat sin, death, and the devil. By putting our faith in Him, we receive forgiveness for our sins and the gift of eternal life.

So, what does faith mean?

Simply put, faith means relying completely on who Jesus is and what He has done to be made right with God.

"HEY, Russell, I see this 'God is bigger' tag you use all the time, but what exactly does it mean? Does that have anything to do with this faith thing you talk about?"

I'm glad you keep asking all these questions, buddy. Let me see if I can explain a little better.

It's more than just a catchy phrase or a wishful hope. It's something I've learned to believe in. Things like this develop in us through trials and experiences. It's the outcomes we see. It's all the times we felt like falling apart but somehow didn't.

By saying, "God is bigger," I'm saying that nothing I face will steal joy from my life. Nothing I go through will be in vain. Although it may suck, I know the Living God I serve is living inside of me; we will face everything together.

Each of us faces problems and, at times, they seem overwhelming. Whether they relate to health, career, finances, relationships, or any other area of life, it can often seem as if our problems are running us over. We may even feel our situations are completely hopeless and that we'll never recover from them.

Trust me, when I heard my doctor utter the word "cancer," I felt as if my days were numbered. But it is in times like those that our faith must be at its greatest. Our faith must become *BIG!*

Our faith should tell us one thing first before anything else: God is the creator of all things and as such, He is bigger than our problems.

That means that nothing happening in our lives is beyond God's control. Faith steps in when you believe that to be true but also seek His help.

We live in a world where we're often told we need to take control of our lives. To some degree, that's true. If you believe in God, you also know that's not entirely possible. Yes, there are many things in our lives we can improve and some problems we can solve. But if God is in control, it follows that we are not. At least not completely.

Sometimes, we just need to step back and try to do our best to view our situations from afar. If we don't understand the problems we're facing, we may be experiencing them for a reason that's simply unknown to us at the moment.

Several possibilities arise:

- God could be trying to prepare us for something bigger in the future.
- He could be trying to humble us as a way to make us better servants.
- He could be working to give us greater empathy for others.
- In order to open a new door to something entirely different, God could be closing the door on something in our past.
- He could be trying to get us to recognize and repent an unconfessed sin.
- God may simply be trying to draw us closer to Him. We're never closer to Him than when we're broken.

It's not easy to do, but it helps if we can try to put our problems into the bigger picture perspective. God may be trying to work out something in our lives we simply don't understand right now. At some point in the future, it may become abundantly clear to us, and we'll realize that what we endured was for our own good.

Praying against what seems to be insurmountable odds is an act of faith, but prayer—in combination with action—can be an even greater act of faith. Praying this way says, "God hasn't answered my prayers yet, but I'm getting myself into position for Him to do just that." Think of it as opening your hand to receive a blessing.

When we take action that's consistent with our prayers, we display faith: God hears our prayers and will answer them. We're going forward, secure in the knowledge that He will meet us along the way.

The word "go" appears in the Bible 1,492 times; the word "stay" appears just thirty-three times. "Go" is an action word. Clearly, our Lord is a God of action.

Now, it is possible we could be charging in the wrong direction, that our actions could be counter to God's desires for us. However, in my experience, even if I'm going in the wrong direction, God seems to make it all work out.

One of my favorite verses is **Romans 8:28 (NIV).** Paul wrote,

> *"And we know that in all things God works for the good of those who love him, who have been called according to his purpose."*

So, if He's working for the good of those who love him, and He's the creator of all things (*bigger* than them all), then surely, He is working on my behalf to use me and my cancer for His glory, which, in my eyes, is the bigger purpose anyway: His glory!

Doctors may want to show me statistics and give me timelines. They may talk about survival percentages and all the "what ifs." God has given me peace about my battle. I believe He's working on my behalf. What He's doing for me, He can do for you no matter your problems! Our faith can lead us to a peace that makes us agree that God is bigger than anything we face.

THE DAY I got the dreaded call, I felt like I should just fall to my knees and yell, "I give up!" Cancer is a scary word. I'd recently lost a good friend to it, and that was still fresh in my mind and heavy on my heart.

Things hadn't been hunky-dory for me at the time either. My doctor was talking to me about my blood pressure. My diverticulitis was flaring up more often. My cholesterol belonged in a KFC bucket, and headaches found me regularly. Now cancer?

Cradling my head in my hands, I sank into a chair at my dining room table. Resting there on my elbows, I wanted to declare defeat. I didn't really want to quit, but it seemed my options had run out.

I'm not sure how many times in my life I've been close to screaming,

"I give up!" but it's been plenty. I'm guessing you've said it, too. Still, one thing is certain for every follower of Christ: Just because we feel defeated doesn't mean we're left for dead. Quite the opposite!

From the depths of our hearts, a little signal pings and fires a rescue flare called *hope*. That's the difference between trusting God and not. Our hope is never lost.

At my dining table that day, hope began bubbling to the surface. Instead of giving up, I found my lips praying a different set of words: *"Jesus, I surrender."*

Nobody likes to raise a white flag. We've been taught that more is better, and failure is not an option.

The world tells us, "You can do it all!" In reality, we can't, nor do we need to. But still, we try.

We overextend our time, overextend our abilities, and overextend our resources. Yet all that overreaching just leaves us gripping the end of our ropes.

I've learned that in those moments swelling with frustration, we have a choice. We can choose to sit with the enemy in defeat, or we can choose to surrender to the Lord in victory. As we surrender to the Lord, our giving up is replaced by His lifting up:

"Humble yourselves, therefore, under God's mighty hand, that he may lift you up in due time. Cast all your anxiety on him because he cares for you." **(1 Peter 5:6-7 NIV)**

As we raise our white flags and cry out to Jesus, He rescues us from the depths. When we humble ourselves before the Lord, we begin to see His mighty hand at work. While we rest safely under God's care, He lifts us up in due time, and His timing is always perfect.

And we didn't really give up! *Surrendering* isn't the same as giving up—not when God is involved.

Submitting to God means humbly placing ourselves at His feet. Then we give up our desire for control and our pride. We give up trying to "fix" it all. Under the care of God's mighty hand, we release the need to know when, why, and how. Faith finds us resting in His power, peace, and provision. This different surrender is a dying of self, and in it, we begin to walk in a fresh, new life with Christ. That walk gives us peace over whatever we're going through.

Whatever your cancer is, whatever your mountain may be, just surrender it. When you do, you must believe that God has taken the wheel. No more questioning, no more doubting. Help is on the way. Hope is bubbling to the surface.

When we find ourselves at the end of our ropes, let's instead cast our anxiety on the Lord. Find peace under the protection of God's mighty hand because He cares for you. Rest there. Don't give up in defeat today. Surrender to the Lord.

SOMETIMES, even after we give it to God, it is human to let things creep back up on us.

Not long ago, I went for my one-year follow-up. I just knew I was going to hear words like "remission;" "free;" "survivor;" and "see you in six months."

Instead, I heard, "See you next week," and "Keep the payments coming."

I went home and tried to do what I usually do to escape the day—write. The only thing was, I didn't know what to write. Just like when this journey began, the words *"God is bigger than"* seemed to shut down my entire thought process. Once again, I was lost as to what should come next, and I wondered why I couldn't finish the thought.

Suddenly, something came over me. That truth hit my heart again, and I knew it covered everything, especially what was consuming those days—fear.

God is bigger than your fear.

Those words echoed in my spirit as I felt the weight of fear begin to lift and the presence of my Father surrounded me with His love. It was so simple yet so remarkably powerful!

The enemy would like us to believe that our fear is bigger than our God. The simple truth of the matter is that it is not. In fact, *nothing* is bigger than our God. Scripture boldly declares it so:

***"Great is our Lord, and abundant in power; his understanding is beyond measure."* (Psalm 147:5)**

Our God cannot be measured. He is great and greatly to be praised. Fear can be quantified to that of our current circumstance, but God is eternal and triumphs over the doings of the devil.

Cousins, this may be one of the simplest devotionals I've ever written, but I believe that's the whole point. Fear tries to complicate. It rears its ugly head to intimidate the children of God into believing it has ground to stand upon. It doesn't.

The truth is, God is bigger than EVERYTHING.

The same God who created a billion stars to lavish you in love and mercy and wash you in truth today is bigger than any mountain in front of you.

That truth is so easy to understand but so hard to put our wholehearted trust in. We are human, and humans tend to complicate everything. If only we could trust God the way we trust our moms and dads when we're young. We think they can fix anything.

Going back to that tightrope walker I mentioned earlier . . .

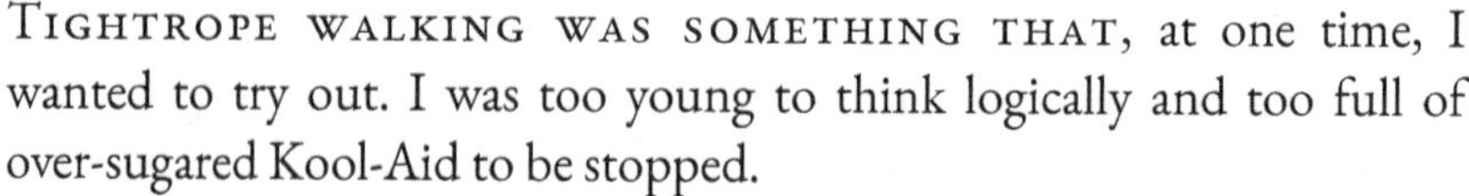

TIGHTROPE WALKING WAS SOMETHING THAT, at one time, I wanted to try out. I was too young to think logically and too full of over-sugared Kool-Aid to be stopped.

We had just watched one of the three channels we could tune in, and the talking heads were going on and on about a tightrope walker in Italy.

"That's what I wanna grow up to do, Dad! I wanna do that so I can be on the news!" I shouted just as the segment cut to some story about a new thing called home computers.

"A computer mechanic? Those things are never gonna catch on. Why on Earth would—"

"No, Dad! A professional tightrope walker!"

"Son, you'd fall off the sidewalk if we didn't hold your hand. You sure this is where you want your college money to go?" Dad asked.

I guess he had a point. We had already saved almost twelve dollars toward college, which meant we had to make good decisions when dealing with that kind of money. So, I thought about it and knew we had to make even better decisions.

"Yep! Positive, Dad!"

"Well, let's get to training. Come on before I change my mind."

Dad dug around in the trunk of his old Nova and pulled out a big yellow tow rope and a set of come-alongs. He tied the rope about six feet off the ground between two trees and tightened it so much the trees bent.

"All right, let's see whatcha got," he told me.

"Don't we need a mattress or pillows under it, Dad?"

"Nah! That takes the fun out of it."

I climbed the rickety boards nailed to the tree that served as my ladder and stood on the rope, still holding onto the tree. I was as nervous as Mike Tyson at a spelling bee. It was only six feet off the ground, but up there, it looked like I was standing on the power lines.

"Dad, will you catch me if I fall?" I asked anxiously.

He replied, "Nope. Gotta learn not to fall. There's nothing to be afraid of if I catch you."

That was "dad logic" that had been handed down through generations upon generations of paraplegics and amputees—a club moms were not allowed to attend.

I took a deep breath. I said a prayer to God and Dale Earnhardt. My knees banged together like valves in a six-cylinder with an oil leak. And then, I let go of the tree.

The rope swayed just a little. I thrust my arms out to balance myself.

"Go on!" Dad encouraged me. "Not gonna make the news standing there with your legs wobbling like that."

He was an expert on encouragement. Maybe a professional . . . or at least all-state, first team.

So, I took a step. Then another. And another. I was doing it! I was about to be newsworthy.

I must have been about mid-way across the rope. I was smiling like I wanted to show off new dentures. It was then that I turned to look at how far I'd gotten—about two feet.

What?!

How? It felt like I'd gone so much farther.

Then . . .

I looked down.

The first rule of tightrope walking is to never look down. Well, that's rule number two. Rule one is don't fall. I managed to break both rules at once!

My feet went above my head. I envisioned Band-Aids and crutches. I closed my eyes and just let it happen, but the ground wasn't near as hard as I thought it would be. I didn't even bounce.

Slowly, I opened my eyes. I was in Dad's arms. He had caught me.

"Thought you said you wouldn't catch me?"

"Can't just watch you break your neck. Besides, all the college money we saved for you would be a waste," he said with a laugh.

As I would learn when I became a dad myself, that translates to, "As long as I'm here to catch you, I'll never let you fall."

Fathers take their jobs seriously. They protect, provide, teach, inspire . . . and they catch. They never let their children fall. As I've learned throughout my life, that applies to our Father in Heaven even more.

The last few months have been nothing less than awful, but God has shown me things I used to overlook. *Every* day is beautiful, and He has shown me that. He's there to catch me when I fall. *Every* time

The Bible tells me to put on my armor. Let my faith stand firm. Go to battle with confidence. I can't let my unfortunate circumstances get in the way of enjoying all of God's blessings, can I?

It also tells me that it's okay to have those not-so-strong moments when I'm weak.

I'm human. Show me a person that says that they never worry, and I'll show you a liar. My mind wonders about all the "what ifs." I plan on having a long, bright, and happy future, but if I listen to the medical professionals, it would be poor planning not to plan for the worst as well. And that's okay.

Planning for the worst doesn't mean I'm discrediting what God can do. It means He's given me enough wisdom to know what to do in such times.

I've been strong for others my entire life, but I have moments when I get blindsided. There's no denying it. I am weak to the core in those moments. My body is tired; it continues to be beaten down by this cuss word named cancer and its devastating effects. Treatments that are supposed to help me feel as if they're destroying me. There are also days when I feel invincible. There are days I feel as good as any day before my diagnosis. There are days I'm reminded that I'm lucky enough to be able to see how God is not just walking with me; I'm riding Him piggyback as I did on my old man.

Those are the days that I know the tightrope wobbled and I closed my eyes . . . and my Father caught me.

If an earthly father is eager to help his son, think of how much more our Heavenly Father is concerned about His children.

In the Old Testament, Moses recalled how God carried His people even as they experienced the danger of faltering faith. He reminded the Israelites of how God delivered them, provided food and water in the desert, fought against their enemies, and guided them with pillars of cloud and fire. Meditating on the many ways God acted on their behalf, Moses said:

"There you saw how the LORD your God carried you, as a father carries his son." **(Deuteronomy 1:31 NIV)**

Life is so unpredictable. Today's dreams for tomorrow can be shattered in a second. We hate to admit it, but we're usually one phone call away from needing to be carried through the next crisis.

Most of us live each day believing *we* are in control, but life has an amazing way of knocking that pride out of our heads. In those moments, we don't know what to do, where to go, or even what to say to God in prayer. So, God carries us. At least God *offers* to carry us.

Some become so filled with the darkness of sudden change that they refuse to let God carry them. They plunge deeper and deeper into the pain of their tragedy, sickness, or loss. It's almost as if they're scared to turn to God because they feel unworthy.

Friend, this is when God tells you to run to Him!

If we believe in our unworthiness, the Bible is filled with folks who didn't deserve His Grace to show us otherwise. They turned to God in great moments of sorrow and pain and discovered the power of God to carry them through the darkness. And guess what? He did!

In life's unpredictable moments, we need God to carry us. We need this more than any other thing that gets us through whatever has us wondering "what if." We must remember that the answer to "Dad, will you catch me if I fall?" is always, "Yes."

That is called faith—when we dig deep and trust our Father. *Faith* and *trust* go hand in hand, and when you learn how they're supposed to be used, it can change your entire life.

I still fall short on days I stress over medical bills and doctor appointments that don't go my way, but can you imagine how missionaries feel? They pick up everything they own and go to a foreign land, sometimes putting themselves in danger, to spread the wonderful news of Jesus. Without having immeasurable faith, they could never gain the trust of new believers.

One such story is amazing to me . . .

LOCATED in the northern deserts of Kenya, you'll find Turkana. It is a land rich in opportunities to minister and experience African culture.

The people have long been plagued with turmoil, harsh conditions, and famines, making them eager to hear good news. A friend of mine, Eddie Williams, is bringing good news.

Eddie is a missionary in Turkana. He's building churches, feeding the hungry, and introducing the Christian gospel to people wanting to hear it.

"Be ready to worship, witness, and get your hands dirty," he'll tell you.

What he does is not for the weak, feeble, or timid. One such obstacle they face routinely is rain, or lack thereof. They sometimes go months without rain. Just before things become critical, prayers are answered. His stories of faith that God will bring the rain are worthy of a book. I hope, one day, he writes about all the great things he's witnessed.

About a year or so ago, I spoke to a lady named Julia Oates.

Like Eddie, Julia developed a passion for spreading God's Word. She visited Uganda, Africa, on two mission trips during her high school years. She grew a passion for Africa and the people there. She will admit, she didn't know much about missionary work in Africa (both historical and current), but she knew it was where God called her, and that was good enough.

Julia also talked about the desperate need for rain in the dry seasons. She told me about one story of faith in particular that's stuck with me. It inspired me to grow my faith.

It had been months since rain last fell. Rivers were dried up. Animals had been driven away in search of water. Villages were on the verge of devastation. *Faith* and *trust* were words that didn't get much mention.

A missionary called all the people in a tiny village to come together to pray. There was only one church within miles, and it was no more than rows of benches lined up outside with no overhead covering, but many people arrived to pray for the needed rain. The missionary greeted most of them as they filed in.

As he walked to the front to officially begin the meeting, he noticed most people were chatting across the aisles and socializing with friends. When he reached the front, his thoughts were on quieting the attendees and starting the meeting. His eyes scanned the crowd as he asked for quiet.

He then noticed a small girl, maybe ten or eleven years old, sitting in the front row. Her face was beaming with excitement. Next to her, open and ready for use, was a colorful and extremely large umbrella, much bigger than her.

The little girl's beauty and innocence made the pastor smile as he realized how much faith she possessed. No one else in the congregation had brought an umbrella. All came to pray for rain, but only the little girl had come expecting God to answer.

That's the kind of faith I want to have. That's the kind of faith we all should strive for.

WHAT STOPS us from having that faith? Is it history that we believe will never change? Is it the assumption that God won't answer our prayers?

More times than not, it is fear.

Fear of trusting. Fear of ridicule. Fear of sacrificing something to show God your obedience. Fear just always gets in the way.

If I could remove something from this world, fear would be at the top of my list. I hate it.

Fear comes in a billion different shapes and colors. Sometimes, it looks like solicitors through a doorbell camera or cell phone bills. Sometimes, it looks like the I.R.S. However, I'm not talking about getting rid of little things like scary bugs, snakes, and 3D movie glasses. I'm talking about important stuff. Stuff that keeps us from believing God is in control. Fear of failure, rejection, or loneliness.

When I was young, no one told me our fears would change from boogie men under our beds to real men in suits. Nobody told me that the biggest things we will fear as we age are the ones we don't see. But it's true, and it only gets worse the older you get.

I used to be afraid of a lot of things, but not the things you'd think.

I wasn't afraid of heights. I climbed the tallest trees I could find. Snakes didn't get me worked up. I used to catch them and keep them in aquariums just for fun. I swam in waters too dark to see in. Fear wasn't found in those things.

What I was afraid of was being homeless. We were always a paycheck away from living in a green Nova. I was afraid of my dad dying. I was afraid of my mom working too much. I was afraid I would let them both down. That terrified me! Even just getting a bad grade set me off because I didn't want them to be disappointed.

Now, my fears are totally different.

I'm still afraid of letting someone down, but they're people that depend on me. I am afraid of dying and leaving them to fend for themselves in a world that's . . . well, scary. I'm starting to fear things like treatments I can't afford and things doctors may miss because they've taken on too many patients and I only get fifteen minutes of their time each visit.

I am afraid we don't talk enough about the things that make us less afraid, about the tokens that take the sting out of being alive. We don't enjoy life because we're too afraid and our boundaries keep us contained.

I wish the news reported more miracles. I wish we found so much enjoyment over the things that do make the news that we hollered about them. Squeal even. I would like for us to forget about fear and instead enjoy Golden Eagle syrup every morning. I wish we celebrated a kid making the A-honor roll with unlimited ice cream.

I wish every human realized we don't have to be afraid. Things will be okay. Everything will work out, no matter what.

If I were in an antique store and came across an old magic lamp with a genie inside, do you know what I'd wish for? First and foremost, I would wish that everyone would come to know Jesus and all the blessings that come with it.

Second, I would wish I could go back in time to meet my heroes in person. Folks like Andy Griffith, Dale Earnhardt, and John Wayne. I would also use that wish to visit my biggest hero. Dad always had time for me whenever I stopped by.

Finally, my third and most important wish would be for *you*—that nobody would ever be afraid again. Not afraid of bad grades, drunk and abusive relationships, failed jobs, or bad transmissions. I would wish it all away.

If I could get a fourth wish, I'd wish that my first wish would make you understand that you already have the authority to gain this promise. We don't have to be afraid, or at least, we don't have to *stay* that way.

Fear keeps you awake at night. It makes you nervous about everything. It steals your life. Fear screws up your digestion and causes Pepto-Bismol stocks to go up. Fear will ruin entire weekends, months, and even years.

So, that's what I would do with my wishes. I would wish them away. Unfortunately, we all know it doesn't work that way.

I have several friends who fear cancer. I have many who have fought it, survived it, and haven't looked back. I've attended funerals for those that cancer took from us. I also have some friends that wouldn't wish it upon their math teachers. I ran into one not long ago . . .

⁂

He was squeezing toilet paper when he hollered my name from twenty feet away. I was comparing the healing properties between brands of canned chili when I heard him.

I hadn't seen him in years. We worked together at one time and shared the same lunch hour. He would show me pictures of hogs he spear-hunted in Arkansas. I showed him how many snack cakes could fit into a six-pack cooler.

When I first met him, we were both so young that we were still stupid. We believed we would live forever. Fear ran from us. We weren't smart enough to be afraid of anything. Now, we're on the downhill side of half a century, and the hill is getting slick. Sleeping wrong scares us. What could be a sore muscle could also be symptoms of a major cardiac event.

He had heard about my cancer through a mutual friend. He beat it himself five years ago.

"It was in my prostate," he told me. "I put off getting checked because my doctor refused to buy me dinner afterward."

My friend finished his treatments. He rang the bell. He whooped and hollered like Ed McMahon showed up at his house with a check the size of Manhattan.

"Do you ever think about, ya know, not winning?" he asked.

"Nah. Not much. Maybe a little. Occasionally," I lied.

I think about it all the time. How can you not? When you hear the word, the first thing you think of is "not winning."

"Man, I was scared senseless," he said, but he used another S-word to prove his point. "Couldn't sleep at night without thinking about it."

Although I do think about it, I've never feared it. I've always been taught to face the things that scare me, to believe in things—good things, like prayer and the curing properties of real love.

People who know me best think I'm not scared of anything. I hate to tell them, but they're wrong. There are a million things I'm scared of. Things I can't control.

First off, I can tell you that I'm not scared of dying. What I have waiting for me is anything but scary. But I am afraid of leaving.

If—a big "if"—I leave this rotating beach ball anytime soon, there's a wife and two youngins that won't have someone here that loves them more than life itself. They won't have the one that sits up at night and prays for them so hard he cries. The one who promised he would always be their biggest fan, fix all their problems, and always hug them the tightest will be gone. That's my biggest fear.

There are other things, too, things that scare the wits out of me when I think about them. Those things don't involve ripping out my emotional piano strings, but I have come to realize they'll change the whole world if something happens to them.

I'm scared all dirt roads will one day be paved. I've seen them give way to tax money like dollar bills were being printed right on Pennsylvania Avenue. Dirt roads are the foundation of your first car. Later in life, they become your therapist. You get a direct line to God when you talk to Him while leaving dust clouds behind you.

I'm afraid old hymnals will one day be extinct. When a choir director stands up front holding a hymnal in one hand and waving the other as if landing a 737, that's when church becomes less religious and more about a relationship.

I'm afraid young boys will one day stop opening doors for young ladies. I'm afraid social media will teach them that self-worth means more than caring for others. "Shares" and "likes" could one day replace homecoming dances and front porch kisses. That would totally wreck teenage boys everywhere.

I'm afraid work boot companies will scale back so they can make room for $300 designer sneakers.

I'm afraid that, before long, dinner tables will no longer be a place for prayer. Even more scary is that dinner tables will no longer be needed at all. Eating in the SUV between two jobs and ball practice will be the new dinner table.

It scares the holy poop out of me that fathers will stop teaching kids to fish. Bass clubs and tournaments are taking the place of cane poles and buckets of crickets. If the above happens, skipping rocks could turn into a bad thing. We might as well cancel *Andy Griffith* reruns altogether.

I'm terrified we'll be made to park our gas-powered vehicles. "Electric energy is the way to go," they're screaming. "Green energy will save the world," they holler.

There's not one electric vehicle that can compare to the feeling of a '67 Camaro screaming down a back road. I don't care if Elon, Deon, or Moron made it; it just can't compare. Years down the road, when batteries occupy landfills, our drinking water will be so toxic our pee will look like the insides of glow sticks.

I'm afraid small country churches will give way to mega-church concerts and preachers that land their jets on private runways. If that happens, there goes potlucks and dinner on the grounds. We might as well turn in our crockpots and baby grand pianos. That leads me back to those hymnals. It's hard to sing "Shall We Gather at the River" over bass drums and electric guitar solos.

What I'm trying to say is that I'm scared this world is changing.

Don't get me wrong. Some change is good. If we hadn't changed over the years, I couldn't watch college football on a seventy-five-inch high-definition flat screen. That's important to me.

I'm also afraid it's changing and removing the things we need. Family time. Prayer time. Small churches that still post the attendance on a slider board.

I'm afraid there will be no need for overalls and porches before long. Tire swings and bicycles will only exist in history books.

You laugh and say it will never happen. Tell that to the *Sears Wish Book*.

So, yes. I am afraid.

I'm afraid of some things, but I am not afraid of cancer. I'm not afraid of "not winning." I'm not afraid this battle will make me ask, "*Why*, God?"

I'm thankful I can instead say, "*What*, God? *What* do you want me to do with this?"

WHEN MY SON WAS LITTLE, we watched a cartoon tomato, asparagus, and cucumber sing a song. It seemed so silly then, but I can remember every word, and it's really not that silly at all.

Its lyrics tell a bedtime tale that many of us faced in our childhoods —that of being tucked into our beds only to discover our surroundings were rather frightening. It sings of creepy monsters, Godzilla, and the dreaded boogie man, but more importantly, the song speaks hope. It boasts a message that literally proclaims that we can call out to God wherever we're scared because He is bigger than any frightening thing we'll ever have to face!

God is bigger than cancer. He's bigger than the cable news guys telling us how horrible the world is. He's bigger than whatever your boogie man is. He's bigger than any mountain you're facing. Everything just seems better when we learn to trust Him each time He says, "Do not be afraid."

Do I think about *it?* Absolutely!

Am I afraid? Not one little bit because God is bigger!

Still . . .

Even those words can't put a forcefield around fear. Fear finds its way in. Faith can help you, but fear lingers. When you find yourself at the cancer clinic, you'll see it tends to loiter there.

Fear really likes to hang out at the UAB O'Neal Cancer Treatment Center in Birmingham, Alabama. I'm there often for scheduled deductible payments and free snacks. There are usually about twenty of my closest warrior buddies there, all fighting to prove somebody wrong.

On one such occasion, the trained professionals were having trouble with my port. Two nurses were involved. They were pushing a needle the size of an Olympic javelin into my chest. They had the combined pushing force of a Peterbilt diesel truck. That was enough to let fear in.

"Are you okay, Mr. Estes?"

"Perfectly fine."

Of course, I was lying. Really, I was trying my best to not throw up.

"Are you sure? You look like you may pass out."

"No, I'm fine."

Again, liar! It was getting to be habitual.

"Can we get you anything?"

"Life insurance," I said.

They finally accessed my port. I started receiving chemicals designed to connect my bank account to their billing department. I could feel money set aside for vacations being directly bluetoothed to some doctor's BMW fund.

Then . . . I waited.

While my treatment worked its magic, I sat in a recliner with buttock warmers, cup holders, and a credit card swipe slot thinking about things to write.

Don't take this the wrong way, but writing is more for me than you. I've got a lot on my mind lately. Stuff that worries me. When I write, my mind can escape. It's the place I go that eases the tension, worry, and stress.

At that moment, I was worried about my wife and kids.

They hold a lot in. They don't like discussing all the things that doctors say can happen. To them, we have one outcome. Nothing more. Plan A is that Dad lives forever. No ifs, ands, or buts. There is no Plan B. Still, I know they think about—y'know—the "other" outcome.

I hate it when they worry. I can't stand it! It makes me sick to my stomach if they suffer at all. I even hate it when they get sinus infections. The worst part is there's not one thing I can do about it, and it's a helpless feeling.

I wish I could take it from them. Just like the Good Lord did for me, I would bear all their worries, pains, and suffering if I could. But I can't. As much as I wish it did, it just doesn't work that way.

So, I write. I think, and I write these awful stories and columns. All they are to me are my thoughts—my winding, pointless, and misspelled thoughts that are a slap in the face to every English teacher I've ever had yet you're all so nice to endure. Some of these collaborations of words even end up in books.

I think about all the things I've used over the course of my life to get me through these types of things. Of course, prayer is my best tool, but I've also used physical places as getaways, like game rooms. Six dollars in quarters and a Miss Pac-Man arcade game is like therapy. Shooting pool can cure pneumonia. Proven fact.

I've also escaped to creek banks when sadness attacked me. There's something about watching a bluegill sink a bobber that helps cure depression. Then there's the Old Faithful of escapes, the one that never fails us: back roads.

There's just something about driving a two-lane highway. I like narrow two-lanes that are shaded by trees. I like old fence posts flying by and my windows down so I can smell the honeysuckles. Old barns that should have been put down years ago; those are fun to see.

Kudzu! I've seen kudzu art on back roads that should be in a museum. Just outside of Fayette, Alabama on Highway 171 stands a kudzu tyrannosaurus rex that was once a wooden light pole. Seeing that prehistoric organic creature makes things better. All things. I don't know why. I can't explain it. Just trust me on this one.

You can't see these things on interstates, but along these little roads, you see things like crippled tractors in front yards. You see stray dogs that are treated like royalty. There are all sorts of things found on back roads that cure common ailments.

It makes me . . . How do I say this? Happy. Peaceful even. It removes a lot of worry.

You have no reason to care about this, but I used to worry a lot more than I do now. I've lost both parents. I've lost my only brother and my only sister. My mother battled dementia. Watching it slowly claim her took a lot out of me. I felt as if it took some of me with it, too.

I've battled my own issues before. Not as bad as what I face now, but, at the time, it was the worst thing ever. There have been a few times that it seemed as if I was worried and afraid of everything, but it wasn't always like that.

It took a lot to scare me as a young boy. I didn't know fear. I'd be the first inside an abandoned house my friends swore was haunted. I'd jump the biggest ramps we could make on a bike made from hand-me-down parts. I was as brave as any kid I knew. Most of the time. However, there were times I was so scared I'd be plum embarrassed if my friends knew. I'd lie in bed and feel so scared I couldn't catch my breath.

Sometimes, I didn't even know what I was afraid of but when I knew, it scared me to the point I called for the Good Lord to just go ahead and take me. I was afraid. Plain and simple. Afraid something would happen to my family. Afraid I would let them down. Afraid I wouldn't be enough for them. I was afraid I would be a failure.

I grew up without a lot of anything. I thought shoes came already broken in and jeans were supposed to be too long, faded, and have a patch on at least one knee. I didn't know any better until I was older. When that time came, I wanted better for my family, but I was scared I couldn't provide. I was a nobody. "Nobodies" don't have better things.

To tell the truth, I was more afraid of the things I couldn't see. I wasn't afraid of bullies, strangers, or tornadoes. You can see those things. It was failure, sickness, worry . . . and yes, death scared me so bad I lost sleep and weight.

Fear has a way of taking over. It finds a crack and slips in. At night, I'd wonder if death was going to swallow me whole. I don't even know why I was so scared of death when I was younger. I was always told that the other side of death was something peaceful and pain-free. But still, there were times I lost sleep thinking about dying.

One day, when I was around the age of twelve, my friend dared me to jump from a bluff into dark water. It was an old strip pit pond, probably only thirty feet or so, but to a kid looking down, it felt like I was jumping from an airplane. I inched up so close to the edge that loose gravel fell into the water below. Then I backed up.

"You chicken?" my friend hollered.

I scooted back to the edge and peered down again. Lord, it must have been a two-thousand-foot drop.

"Go on!" he shouted. "I double-dog dare ya."

He was such an inspirational speaker, my friend was. He then made the clucking sound of a chicken, indicating he was going to let it be known in school that I was a big wuss. The double-dog dare took me to the edge, but the sound of that clucking produced more bravery in me than a fifth of whiskey did for my underage cousins.

As I peeked down at the water, I imagined free-falling for at least twenty-five minutes and asked God to give me the courage. I turned around, gazed at my friend, and smiled. Then I jumped! It was terrifying, but I did it.

Neither of us said much. He couldn't believe I'd done it. I couldn't either. But I did, and it did something to me. I escaped into a world where failure was no longer a word. I lived in the moment.

Seeing me do it, my friend followed suit. He splashed down like a watermelon falling from the top branch of the watermelon tree. We swam for hours, laughed and shouted and hollered like we'd just won the state championship. We escaped! We lived! You know what else we did? We proved we were not afraid.

I felt something that day. I wish I could tell you I felt less afraid, but that wasn't it. I felt sort of strong. Feeling strong can make fear easier. Being strong counts for a lot. The more you go through in life, the stronger you get, and that experience takes the place of fear.

I still wonder what lies ahead for me. I've got more hope than I had just a couple of months ago.

They say these treatments could be my "miracle."

I know better. Miracles don't come from doctors. Miracles come from the Big Guy you talk to when you're standing on the edge of a bluff and you want your friend to stop making chicken noises.

⸺⦿⸺

THERE'S A NEW "SOMETHING" I've been told about. It's deep—between my liver and lungs. It's too risky to remove through surgery, so we're going to let these treatments pick a fight with it and, in the words of the doc, "See what happens."

Does it worry me? A little.

Am I afraid? No. I'm ready to jump!

But I'm not gonna lie to you. I'm tired. More so achy *and* tired. Gosh, I'm so, so tired.

I've tried everything to give me energy. I have friends who have suggested everything from mineral oils to Native American tribal dances. I've Googled home remedies and folklore medicine to the extent that I feel like the feds will bust in at any minute and arrest me for running an illegal health clinic.

But I feel like I'm over the hump. I feel like I'm going to beat this cuss word inside me.

Am I scared? I think I'm more worried. Not about anything I can see but something way more important. I'm worried about the people I love because they're worried about me.

That's why I smile so much. Smiles hide things, things that make you lie awake at night and cry when nobody knows.

On the table beside my living room chair is a Bible, one just like my momma and daddy clinched between their hands many times when they were standing on the edge of a cliff, ready to jump—but still scared.

That Bible reminds me that the fella writing this is stronger than he knows. All these warriors I see at treatment centers are stronger than their cancer ever thought about being.

The same goes for you.

I don't know who you are, where you're right now, what kind of private hell you're going through, or how big the mountain you're climbing is. You may be battling your own cancer called another name, like depression, anger, a failed relationship, or financial hardship—

anything that's pushed you to the edge. You're standing there, looking down at the water. You want to jump but you're afraid.

Please trust that some fella you may have never even met did his best to write this for *you* to remind you . . .

It's okay to be afraid, but don't forget how strong you are. Remember that the bigger your faith is, the less fear will find you.

CHAPTER 14

I'M POSITIVE THAT I WILL BE POSITIVE

Staying positive is one of the greatest challenges of life, especially for cancer patients and caretakers. It's certainly a huge challenge for me and my wife Kristy during our stage four melanoma cancer battle which began over a year ago.

Between the cancer prognosis and side effects of the "cures," negativity was my default outlook. But God (don't you just love that phrase—"But God"), who makes streams in the middle of deserts, consistently broke through the fog of my cancer battle to deliver His positivity!

Leaning on His Word and my faith, I began to make decisions that not only promoted positive energy, but I learned I had to cut out negative vibes. Sadly, that included some people. God will surround us with who we need during our troubled times, but we must make sure we make room for those people.

In life, everything you do starts with a choice you make.

Do you choose to wake up positive, or do you choose to spew negativity? Do you choose to be thankful for another chance to open your eyes and take a breath, or do you just jump out of bed every morning as if it's yet another day you deserve?

Being thankful and positive can not only change your outlook but the outlooks of those around you.

Though I wouldn't wish cancer on anyone, I long for my brothers and sisters in Christ to experience firsthand what happens when we accept the reality of our circumstances and not only trust God but thank Him for the path He's laid out for us.

I'm even thankful for these dark times. Yes, they may be stressful, but we can find reasons to be thankful through any hard season. I can honestly say that I have grown more intimate with Christ because of what I've endured. A greater sense of His faithfulness is a prime example.

When I cried out to Him from my bed in the middle of the night, He was already there, calming my broken heart and assuring me of His love, just as His Word tells us:

"Your love, LORD, reaches to the heavens, your faithfulness to the skies." **(Psalm 36:5 NIV)**

A richer understanding of His peace has come from this cancer battle. After the oncologist explained my diagnosis, the Lord dried my tears and reminded me of His sovereignty in all things. Since God's in charge and we are not, we can let go of our anxious thoughts and rest in Him:

"And the peace of God, which transcends all understanding, will guard your hearts and your minds in Christ Jesus." **(Philippians 4:7 NIV)**

A constant assurance of His goodness finds us. Because His plans for us are always good and always purposeful, I can lift my head and say,

> *"I remain confident of this: I will see the goodness of the LORD in the land of the living."* (Psalm 27:13 NIV)

A deeper dependence on His presence is now something that I not only need but expect. That's what He wants—expectation. Desperately aware of my need for Jesus, I am praying more often and more earnestly than ever before. When I'm on my knees, He meets me without fail. Thus, everyone should:

> *"Devote yourselves to prayer, being watchful and thankful."* (Colossians 4:2 NIV)

I've witnessed a fresh experience of His freedom. Of all the emotions that have washed over me, true fear held sway for only one terrible day. After much weeping and gnashing of teeth, by God's grace, I chose to stand on His truth and be set free:

> *"So do not fear, for I am with you; do not be dismayed, for I am your God."* (Isaiah 41:10 NIV)

I have a clearer vision of His hope. Whatever the outcome—healing or Heaven—God holds out a bright beacon of hope for my future *and yours*, and He provides the greatest reason for gratitude, evidenced here:

> *"Therefore, since we are receiving a kingdom that cannot be shaken, let us be thankful . . ."* (Hebrews 12:28 NIV)

As much as God has shown me, I just know that there is so much more that's waiting. I feel Him leading me. When His answer is, "Not yet," I know it doesn't mean "not at all."

There are days I wish the answer for my healing was, "Right now!" but seeing what He has already done for me calms my spirit.

SOME MORNINGS ARE JUST DOWNRIGHT bad. I often wake with terrible headaches. Cancer treatments have damaged my adrenal glands, and this, as the doctor puts it, "is just part of it."

On these mornings, I don't want to do anything except drink my coffee and sit in darkness. As much as I love my morning devotional and time in God's Word, even they are in jeopardy. Usually, just as the sun finds its way over the trees lining our property, I start reading. Then I read a little more. Before long, I finish my devotional, then I read other passages and usually end up with one of the best mornings with God.

Why? Because I'm staying obedient . . . and He hugs me. He wraps His arms around me when I'm feeling tired, weak, and broken.

Does my pain go away? No, but I don't dwell on it any longer.

Am I tired? I feel like I haven't slept in weeks, but I'm reminded that I'm not alone in this race.

We all struggle with spiritual discouragement and lethargy. Mine hits me like a ton of bricks the days following treatment. Some days, our circumstances threaten to overwhelm us, and we struggle just to pray. Many times, we simply don't feel like doing the things we know we should. For one reason or another, God sometimes seems far off and unreachable. But He's not. He's right here with you.

On the mornings like I wrote about above, I like to read from the Psalms. I love the songs and praises.

In his life, David faced times like you and I are experiencing. The Psalms are filled with verses that express his despair and feeling of abandonment. Yet the Psalms also give us the key to living victoriously during life's dark periods:

"Forever, O Lord, Your word is settled in heaven. Your faithfulness continues throughout all generations; You established the earth, and it stands. They stand this day according to Your ordinances . . ." (Psalm 119:89-91 NKJV)

My circumstances or feelings have not changed how I see God. He is the same God today as He was when He hung the stars in the sky, led the Israelites through the Red Sea, and fed the five thousand.

". . .For all things are Your servants." (Psalm 119:91 ESV)

All things, even the things affecting me right now, are God's servants. The circumstances, people, and events around me are all under God. They are His servants, designed to help and bless me spiritually.

"If Your law had not been my delight, Then I would have perished in my affliction. I will never forget Your precepts, for by them You have revived me. I am Yours, save me; For I have sought Your precepts. The wicked wait for me to destroy me; I shall diligently consider Your testimonies." (Psalm 119:92-95 NIV)

Recalling God's faithfulness and control over everything that touches us will give us strength to walk with God even when we feel like giving up in despair. After all, our feelings and circumstances have not changed God. He is perfectly capable of sustaining us if we will only let Him. We simply need to choose to keep chasing God despite how we feel.

Choosing to stay positive might not be easy. It might even involve hard work. But only God can revive and save our souls from spiritual lethargy. When you feel spiritually drained or inadequate, remember that you have a choice. You can wrap yourself up in excuses and self-pity, or you can choose to draw your strength from an unchanging God.

I FEEL as if God talks to me more when I forget the excuses and just "be still" so He can speak. That's where I often find my writing material. I can take a very uneventful morning and write a devotional so long I get a warning from Facebook. I put together words I didn't know I could afford.

I've long been a collector of words. Whether writing or speaking, I use certain words to change the mood and atmosphere. Words can do that! I've always appreciated how words play with my thought process, give me insight into someone else's mind, and often bring a new perspective to an old idea. The meaning and interpretation behind words have always been a welcome challenge to me.

What I love most though is that words can provide encouragement or motivation to make today count; or for anyone searching for a little bit of light on a dark day, this is for you. Let me give you some words:

Begin each day with a grateful heart. – Roy Bennett

This simple statement is a great way to start your day. Expressing your gratitude on a regular basis is like taking a daily supplement of vitamins. An attitude of gratitude has a positive effect on your mental health, brain function, and overall well-being. Choosing gratitude makes everything a little better.

Don't let someone else's opinion of you become your reality. – Les Brown

How often do you let the grumpy store clerk influence your day? Getting set off when someone's attitude rubs you the wrong way is easy. Don't internalize and let your thoughts take you off on some new reality trip. Choose to let their opinion slide off of you. Say, "No thank you" and walk away.

It's never too late to be what you might have been. – George Eliot

This one is one of my favorites! If I didn't believe this, I'd still be trying to figure out what to do with my life. Your past is your past, and your future is still waiting for you to make it. Too often we allow our past to determine what we think we can or cannot do. Keep focused on what you want to do and make it happen. Persistence, determination, and vision make a recipe for success.

Just as you can feed off words, you can use them for others. Choose kind words. Choose words to inspire and motivate. Choose to be the reason someone smiles. Words can do that! Words are powerful and when used in prayer, they can become amazing things.

Prayer is something on which I have relied. I definitely needed it for this mountain climb. Praying has helped me more than I can explain. It has made me feel better on days that haven't gone my way. No . . . actually, it is better than that—I'm blessed! And *blessed* ranks a lot higher than *feeling better*.

I tend to worry when I have scans and other tests that update me on how well the treatments are working against the cancer, but I know without a doubt that my prayer warriors are going to battle during those times. I always hope for the best results, and I know those prayers play a part in that. If the treatments are doing their job, I'm winning the battle. If not . . .

Well, let's not mention the "if not." There is no "if not." The treatments must be working.

My mind works overtime on this stuff. I know my God is bigger; I'm at peace with whatever His plan is, but I think about it all. I wouldn't say I'm worried now, but I do get anxious. Still, I consider myself a blessed man.

God chose me to do His work through this battle. I plan on doing just that—with a smile. Whatever I do for the Lord, I do with gratitude. Besides, there are tons of folks worse than me who are fighting this awful cuss word. As long as God allows me to, I'm gonna live life to the fullest.

I REMIND myself that our lives don't stop because we had a bad day. A bad day by the standard you and I have could be the best day in a long time for someone else. What about the homeless, the incarcerated, the abused, or the hungry? When we think of the many circumstances we could be faced with, we tend to put in perspective what a bad day really is. We still have blessings all around us that many in this world will never see.

We must deal with our issues during the days filled with anxiety, but it is also up to *you* to turn *your* day around. Don't rely on a friend or spouse to "make things better." Sure, their prayers make an impact when they shout to Heaven on your behalf. But *you* have to create a "positive," even if you have to force yourself, and you'll be surprised at how much better things get.

Even on my bad days, I try to compose something that may help someone else. A story, a devotion, maybe a simple quote. It doesn't have to be published. A simple message to a friend is always positive.

Some of the most noted people in the Bible created good from bad. The Apostle Paul composed Philippians while he was in prison. It turned out to be one of the most uplifting books in the Bible, including one of my favorite passages:

"Do not be anxious about anything, but in every situation, by prayer and petition, with thanksgiving, present your requests to God. And the peace of God, which transcends all understanding, will guard your hearts and your minds in Christ Jesus." **(Philippians 4:6-7 NIV)**

That Paul was able to reject anxiety, even during his imprisonment, makes this passage all the more encouraging.

Our days travel at the speed of sound. The older you get, the faster they go. They tend to go by even faster when there's no positivity in your life, but you're stuck in the mud when those negative vibes fill your head.

"Life is short!"

You hear that a lot, but is it?

"It seems like only yesterday that (fill in the blank) was just a baby."

We hear that a lot, too; even things like, "Whaddaya mean mullets are back in style? They never left!"

The truth is that life is as much as you make it. If you're blessed to live out a life to the average expectancy, that's a long time. You should see several presidential terms, advancements in technology, and at least a million new versions of smartphones. So, why do we say life is short?

It's not life that's short but the *moments in our lives* that are short.

Ah, now we're getting somewhere.

Your kids, if you have them, for example . . . Those are moments you cherish. You love the little things they did growing up and you remember each one so vividly that "it seems like it was yesterday."

As a new mom or dad, nights are long. You sleep very little. You remind yourself, *This won't last forever.* You tell yourself, "It will get better." Then, one day, they're driving away to their own place to live.

Even as you make new memories, those times that weren't so fun still often rush back. You remember how you would sit, tired and sleepy but holding that baby. And you smile.

What about bad memories? What occupies those? Loss of jobs? Death? Broken relationships?

What about friends? Do you have friends that fill your moments, good and bad? Or do you let envy, gossip, or perhaps even hate get in the way of creating friendship memories?

I use social media to do much of the promotion when I release a new book. In the past, even though I asked several times, I couldn't get as much as a "like" let alone a "share" from some *friends*. I didn't ask them to buy the book. I only wanted them to "help out a friend." After all, sharing a book ad should have been as easy as sharing the politician memes they posted to their pages twenty times a day, right? Well . . .

Do I dwell on that? No! If I valued friendship on social media "likes" and "shares," the initial value I placed on that friendship was in a bad place.

What about money? Debt? Do you have friends who owe you money?

If I collected all that was owed to me, I could buy you all lunch today. Here's my thought on that:

You did your part by helping a friend. It's up to them to hold up their end of the deal. If they don't? You can still be friends; you just know where you stand on their side . . . and you won't loan them money or sell them an item for which they say they'll "pay you later" ever again.

The point is that placing more value on possessions and money than actual friendships will steal your moments.

Believe it or not, I've even had people—my *"friends"*—use my cancer battle for their personal benefit. They used my circumstances to self-promote by attaching my name and my struggle to their own causes, which had no connection to me or what I'm going through.

Dwell on it? Nope!

Get mad? Not a chance.

Learn something about them? You betcha!

Allowing that to steal even a moment of happiness from me is giving away minutes that I could be happy, smiling, and helping others.

So, is life short? Not at all.

Moments are short, and you either fill them with positive energy or allow anger, hate, greed, or a number of other negative things to fill the space instead.

Choose kindness in every instance. Be a good friend, even to those that don't hold you as high on their value chart. After all, life can be short, but only if you let it be.

———··◁◯▷··———

NOT LONG AGO, I encountered a man who put the value of life in perspective for me. He caused me to think hard about all the things we're blessed with, even while going through bad times.

I first met Jim via a cellular phone. His daughter was the one who told me I should meet him. Jim is battling pancreatic cancer, but he doesn't trust people until he sees how they fish. So, we planned to go fishing.

We met one day at one of the best "life discussion" places ever invented. There I was, at the water's edge, with my new buddy. Jim was catching fish. I was untangling fishing line. He was on his third keeper of the evening. I was on my second reel because the first one gave up the spirit and went to live with Poseidon.

I cast, untangled line, got caught on sunken logs, and mumbled words that cost me money in the Baptist offering plate. Jim was silent and stayed busy setting hooks on bass the size of Christmas hams. At that point, I could tell his trust issue was going to be a problem.

"Doctors telling you all sorts of horror stories too, I hear," he said over the sound of me pulling in tree limbs.

"Yep. But I'm gonna keep believing they're wrong," I told him.

"Why is that?" he asked.

Now, why in the world did he have to ask me that?!

I didn't know how to answer. I froze. I was six casts, two reels, and six tree limbs into the conversation. Based on how my fishing was going, I figured I wasn't going to gain Jim's trust but I didn't want to run him off before I broke my line again.

"They told me treatment was up to me," he said. "Stage four, and it's aggressive. May or may not help me at this point. Good Lord knows when my number is up. If it's my time, He's gonna get me no matter what. Not sure I want to go through all that chemo mess."

I remained silent. I sensed he wasn't done, and I didn't want to pull out in front of him. So, I cast again and sat my hook on a sunken log. It was a keeper.

"Folks don't appreciate what the Good Lord gives them until it's too late," Jim explained as he pulled in another water hog. "If we learn to appreciate every day and not worry so much about the 'what ifs,' things wouldn't bother us near as much."

He turned to show me his newest trophy. I lifted a tree branch and grinned.

"We get in the way of ourselves too much," Jim said. "Sometimes, we just gotta give it to God and go fishing."

That's me in a nutshell. I worry so much that I can't fish. I worry about getting hung on logs. I worry about where to cast. I worry about the "what ifs." This cancer is no different. It needs to be left at God's feet so He can do his work and we can "catch fish."

WHY DO we try to limit God? I find myself asking—and unfortunately, doing—this a lot.

As I've prayed and (more importantly) listened over the past few months while battling this cuss word, I've found myself to be Public Enemy #1 when it comes to this mindset. It hasn't been intentional on my part but more of a byproduct of my "I want to be in control" Type-A human nature. It's a cross between preachers and bootleggers. I carry the gene.

This is probably more volatile than the most potent Molotov cocktail you can imagine. When I finally shut my mouth and just listened, crazy things began to happen. When I gave into God's voice and surrendered all I am to give Him control, I had such a sense of clarity.

I remember a talk I had with my cousin Shane a few years ago. He had come to my house to look at a little car I was selling.

Shane was having really bad back issues at the time. He couldn't do many of the things he was used to doing. Even the trip to my house almost put him down like a dehydrated tomato. Still, he was as happy and joyful as a fat kid at a tent revival dessert table.

I was venting about my problems and worked up because of issues with two of my friends. They were feuding like a squirrel and a hound over a dispute that didn't even make sense. I'd tried to mediate. That went about as well as a Jehovah's Witness showing up at a Presbyterian open house.

"Man, they just won't listen!" I hollered. "And I don't want either of them mad at me over this."

He just laughed at me. "Cuz, I don't care about what people think. I just do what's right, thank God for what He's given me, and let the rest roll off my back."

"That's hard to do," I replied.

"Not really. It's not hard at all if you truly believe what you're praying to Him about. If you're doing anything else, you're not praying. You're just talking."

RECALLING that story makes me think about the question Jim asked me . . .

I don't know why I believe the doctors are wrong. Maybe because I believe the God I serve is bigger than cancer. Even if that is the reason, what led to it?

Well, I guess I've seen firsthand how He can intervene and make bad things good.

I recently talked to another man who survived cancer. You may say that's not noteworthy. People survive cancer all the time. True, but this guy was given less than six months to live. Doctors wrote him off. That was eight years ago.

"How'd ya beat it?" people often ask him.

He replies, "Me? I can't beat anything . . . but God can."

I've seen God in other places, too. Places that may not seem worthy of telling you about. I'm not good at determining this stuff anyway, so here goes.

I've seen an orphan find a home with a couple that couldn't have kids. That kid breathed new life into them, and they made that kid believe that people really do love others. It changed their entire lives.

They're as happy as a Siamese cat in a catnip factory. They don't even remember life without each other, mainly because there wasn't.

I watched a woman marry a man and be happy. You say there's nothing extraordinary about that, but you don't know the rest of the story, the part where she was alone for twelve years. She was scared to even date. She once ran out of a Red Lobster because a guy smiled at her. That was because her first husband was abusive.

She spent nights in emergency rooms, lying about falling and burning herself on the stove. She had been broken and abused for so long that she didn't believe it would ever change. Then she met someone. He knew she was fragile. He took his time . . . gave her space . . . and never went to Red Lobster. Now, she calls him her husband and meets him at the door every day when he gets home. He holds her before he even sets his lunch bucket down. She feels safe and feels loved. She believes again.

I know a guy who lost his son. He was taken home at age twenty. God called his name before his father was ready to give him up. The dad was broken. He was a shell. He almost ended his own life. But he found the Bible. He found a purpose. He found a reason to smile again.

That father now organizes charity events. He's a life coach who shows others that life has so much to offer that it's ridiculous if we don't find a way to shine in this world. He is a positive energy that helps other parents who have lost kids. I've seen it. It's amazing!

I believe in good things. I guess that's why I believe doctors are wrong when they tell me bad news.

I believe God will put together two people who are fighting cancer and let them go fishing. Two guys who were strangers. Two guys who believe in good things. And the day I met Jim, we talked about things I'm not at liberty to tell you about, but those things were needed.

Look, I'm gonna shoot straight with you. Through this battle, this fight, this war, this *climb*, I've been all over the board with my feelings. I've been fighting this mess for over an entire year. When my journey started, doctors assured me I'd be done with it by now.

I guess when that milestone came and went and I was still fighting, it made me wonder how much longer I could continue. Then I thought about what my cousin Shane told me , and I thank

God for what He's given me and let the rest roll off my back. And I trust Him.

How much longer can I do this? As long as He needs me to. That's how long. Sometimes, we just gotta give it to God and go fishing.

I KNOW that as long as I trust God and allow Him to use me to find glory in all this, it will all work out. I will have healing, either here or in Heaven.

There is so much I've learned in the last year of my life. I have learned I have some really good friends. I learned some of the ones I thought were really good friends are not.

I've learned to be okay with not being in control of things. No matter how hard I work or what I do, I cannot control people, outcomes in ministry, others' choices, or unexpected turns in my health. There is no formula in Scripture that will guarantee desired outcomes if I simply do the "right thing." I must deal with the illusion of self-determination and the idol of control and learn to trust the God of everlasting mercy and goodness.

I hope there's a lot more still waiting for me. It has been an unexpected and, at times, frightening medical journey, but God is teaching me many heart lessons through this confrontation with cancer. These lessons are ongoing chapters in a much longer story God is writing with my life.

I am not nearly as strong as I imagine myself to be. I am not nearly as wise as I perceive myself to be. I am not nearly as self-sufficient as I pretend.

As a broken sinner, I'm weak, foolish, needy, and dependent. I cannot handle life on my own, neither the good times nor the tough times. I *need* God and His grace and mercy constantly, but by the grace of God, I am what I am.

1 Corinthians 15:3 affirms that His grace toward me was not in vain. Because of that, I can choose to be faithful, hopeful, and positive.

I'm not so sure the most important sort of healing is physical. When God looks at me, I suspect He doesn't see cancer as my most serious problem. I believe cancer entered my life by the sovereign will of God. It wasn't a random accident. I take great comfort in trusting He permitted my cancer to achieve some deeper, eternal purpose. God will use the broken things of this sin-cursed world to accomplish His will for my good and His glory.

1 Corinthians 12:9 promises me that His power is made perfect in weakness and that He who began a good work in me will bring it to completion on the day of Jesus Christ **(Philippians 1:6)**.

And what is this good work? **Romans 8:29** affirms that it is to be conformed to the image of His Son.

In **Hebrews 2:9-10**, Christ displayed the grace of God through suffering. Through suffering, I can know Christ better, and I can become more like him **(Philippians 3:10)**.

Jesus promised He would build his church in **Matthew 16:18**. God *will* accomplish His work of redeeming a people from every tribe and tongue **(Revelation 5:9; 7:9-10)**. That is not in doubt.

I'm privileged to have a small role in the big story He's writing. I'm not the center of the story, and its successful ending doesn't hinge on my skills or talents. I must not take myself too seriously. It is a remarkable testament to His power that He's able to accomplish anything through me:

"We have this treasure in jars of clay, to show that the surpassing power belongs to God and not to us." (2 Corinthians 4:7 ESV)

Life is brief, and I should not take my days for granted:

"For you are a mist that appears for a little time and then vanishes." (James 4:14 ESV)

I should do today the things that have lasting value. I should stop so that I can hear people's stories. I should spend time—unhurried and undistracted—with my wife, kids, and my friends and cousins. I should be present with the people God brings into my life. I should take each day as a gift from His hand.

My source of contentment must be Jesus alone, but I'm discovering I have a much greater propensity to seek joy and contentment in people and things other than Jesus. For example, if my health were taken from me, could I be content? What about other people and things precious to me—my family, my work, my financial resources, my reputation? Would Jesus be enough for me if those were gone?

I am learning that suffering is a gracious gift from God that strips away all that competes for my affections and loyalty to Him. Now I can begin to understand and live in the truth of the Word:

"For to me, to live is Christ, and to die is gain." **(Philippians 1:21 NIV)**

And I am still learning *all* these things.

Most learning requires a longer process than most of us expect. God breaks through the ingrained patterns of thought and behavior we developed over many years. My list of lessons learned is always growing; sometimes daily.

Some days, these lessons seem crystal clear, and I accept them. On other days, I have many questions that propel me to probe deeper into those lessons. However, I hope in the truth of **Psalm 138:8 (ESV):**

"The LORD will fulfill his purpose for me; your steadfast love, O LORD, endures forever. Do not forsake the work of your hands."

A growing and changing faith doesn't always translate to a spiritually painless life. Having faith is easy when life is nearly perfect. But when difficulty and pain arise, faith can be hard—and that's okay.

In those times when life turns upside down, remember this: Faith is possible, faith is sometimes painful, and faith can be the one thing that pulls you through. With all its tragedies and ambiguities and sudden, startling joys, faith is what makes life bearable.

Faith and belief go hand-in-hand. When in crisis, your beliefs can get jostled around, but your faith can be the steadying factor. Yes, faith can be challenged but I have found that faith also sustains us while all else is being questioned, including long-held beliefs.

Hope and gratitude are the foundations of faith. Hope can stare down any diagnosis. Hope allows for tears and laughter. Hope looks forward when all else tells us to give up. Our gratitude for what God can, has, and will do in our lives makes us not only thankful for His work in us but for the outcome we believe awaits us.

Optimism, on the other hand, is temporary and easily poked full of holes when life gets difficult. Faith—built on hope and gratitude—is enduring.

As one cancer survivor said to me, "I hope God doesn't see my faith as weak because I feel so down. I'm really struggling."

I assured her that God has no expectation that her faith results in keeping her happy all the time. I also assured her that especially during her time of struggle, mercy abounds—even when optimism goes missing.

Perhaps it can even be said that your faith is weakest when you feel strong on your own and strongest when you feel weak. Faith may be like a mighty oak that never bends to gale-force winds, or it may be like a tiny seed being nurtured beneath, ready to burst open with hope and joy on another day. I've seen people who claimed to have the strongest faith ponder their very worth. I've also seen other people who thought they were faithless reach deep within and find something new and sustaining.

One thing all this has taught me is that God can take something that was supposed to wreak havoc on us and turn it into something amazingly beautiful.

The day cancer showed up in my life, God showed up bigger. He served up a portion of His presence, enough for one day. Enough to reassure me I'm not alone. He's done the same a hundred times over each and every day that's followed.

Cancer may not be your mountain. It may be one of the many things in life that cripple us. Whatever you're going through, just know that the mountain you're facing was put there not to break you, but to grow you into something you never knew you could be.

That mountain may be big . . . but *God is bigger!*

EPILOGUE

A lot has happened since I first started writing this book. I have grown in my relationship with my Lord and Savior so much that it seems as if I'm an entirely different person. It's not that I wasn't following and chasing God before, but I think I found a new summit I didn't know was reachable.

See, I've encountered many *false* summits throughout my life. Let me explain . . .

Growing up teetering on the fence of poverty, I was ecstatic when I landed my first big job. I was getting paid more than I ever thought was possible. I'd never had credit awarded to me like it was then, and it consumed me. I bought everything I wanted because it came with a payment plan that I could do.

For the first time in my life, I had a new truck. I bought a house. I was spending time with God daily, and I felt like life could not get any better. I just knew I was standing on the peak of the mountain! Or at least I thought I did.

I started to grow discontent with things happening at the company where I was employed. I was no longer happy going to work. I'd allowed my new pay scale to cause me debt. As things ate at me, I began realizing that what I *thought* was the pinnacle of my life was no mountaintop. It wasn't any more than a slowly crumbling ledge I had chosen to camp out on and enjoy the earthly rewards of.

The worst part was that I'd started distancing myself from God. Where God wanted to take me was much higher than I wanted to go; I quit climbing. I spent less time in His Word. I could look up, but I couldn't see the summit. I was stuck, hanging on a ledge, wondering what rock to grab onto next. All along, my Rock was reaching down for me.

That's kind of where I am now.

I learned this cancer battle had me on a false summit. Just as I felt as if I were only a few steps away from planting my flag, I looked up and saw there was much, much more mountain above me.

On what would have been my fourth treatment in New York, I found myself unable to make the trip from Alabama to the Big Apple. I contracted the COVID-19 virus and became very sick. I couldn't fly. The airlines wouldn't let me. Even if I had felt like making the grueling sixteen-hour drive, I wouldn't have been allowed to undergo the treatment itself.

Due to it being a clinical trial, my timeline for treatments was vital to the data the research team was collecting. Once my data was unique and different from the group I was in, it wouldn't be able to be used for research. So, I was expelled from the trial.

That was like taking a punch in the gut. All my wind was gone, and I was just sitting on my ledge wondering whether I should keep climbing.

I felt I'd done my best to climb my mountain. I thought the summit was so, so near. But I was stuck. Again. And it got worse.

A few weeks later, I underwent exams that showed the trial was working. The number of cancer cells was drastically reduced from where they were at the beginning of the trial. Had I been able to continue the treatments, my cancer would have become much more curable—or at least given me a much better chance of remission. Receiving that news made my trial expulsion even tougher to accept.

In a nutshell, it seemed the trial was saving my life, but I could no longer be a part of it. That hurts! I think I would have been better off not knowing.

As this book comes to completion, more new areas of concern have shown up. There is another tumor that looks to have metastasized. All the scans and lab work point to it being the cuss word. A biopsy has not yet been completed, but here I am, once again, on my ledge.

So, what am I going to do?

I'm already climbing.

On the days that I'm tired, I rest. As soon as my strength is restored, I lift my hand toward the heavens and my God grabs it. He pulls me up. Then I reach up and grab the next ledge.

I do not look down. That lesson has already been learned! I am not concerned with where I've been. Instead, I focus on where I'm going, and where I'm going is the ultimate summit.

I will keep pushing. I will keep climbing. I may even encounter more false summits along the way. I've realized that as long as I keep climbing, I *will* one day plant my flag on that peak and I will declare victory!

I will conquer the mountain, and I will stand with nothing else above me except my God! Not chemo. Not immunotherapy. Not a trial. Victory will be mine because the battle belonged to the Lord. It was always His—just as I am, have been, and always will be. Either way, I win.

As I get ready for this book's release, I pray that each word in it is not *from* me, but *through* me, from the best Mountain Trail Guide that you will ever have as you climb your mountain. I am praying for people I don't even know . . . the ones that will pick this up and read it, the ones that are climbing and want to give up. I am praying you don't and instead, you find the strength to keep climbing.

I'm still climbing. At times, I feel as if this mountain is untamable. That's when I dig deep. That's when I reach out my hand, and I take a step. I know I'm not climbing alone.

This mountain is huge. It is so, so huge. But I'm climbing because of the faith I have in knowing one thing about the circumstances of the mountain: It may be big, but ***GOD IS BIGGER!***

9 798218 273002